WILLIAM & MARY

Mary King

DAVID & CHARLES

Contents

Foreword *by Lord Patrick Beresford*   8

Love at First Sight: *The early years*   10

Life as a Superstar: *The highlights*   28

Family, friends & fans   80

Home life in Salcombe Regis   104

William's Triumphs: *The statistics*   121

Foreword *by Lord Patrick Beresford*

Chef d'Equipe to the British Team 1985-92

If you are inclined, as I am, to rate an eventer at first sight by how pleased you are to find it waiting for you at second horses on a Quorn Friday or a Beaufort Saturday, then inevitably King William would come out very near the top. Not only has he got terrific scope and physique, but also what is sometimes called 'the look of eagles', that is to say an imperious eye which, rather than focusing on his near surroundings, seems to be searching for a pack of hounds on the distant horizon, or perhaps even in those Elysian fields which lie beyond.

That, anyway, was the impression he gave me on the first occasion that I can consciously remember seeing him, namely at the 1991 Badminton trot-up. That year an unlucky fall on the flat in Huntsman's Close robbed him of a clear round. However, by winning the British Open at Gatcombe the following August, he earned himself the accolade of being given the number three position in running order for our team at the Punchestown Europeans a month later.

Mary and he were in the lead after the dressage. and I can well recall watching them, from the top of a bank near the ten-minute box, stride around the cross-country in remorseless rhythm, devouring the fences with almost contemptuous ease, absolutely spot-on by the clock, until an over-bold leap into the water at the third last tipped them up. King William was quickly caught and taken back for Mary to remount and complete – in a time still faster than many who had gone clear.

That evening he required four stitches in his near fore but nevertheless trotted out sound the next morning – for which much credit is due to Annie Collings, his tireless girl groom, and to Paul Farringdon, our team vet. Mary was less lucky, having torn the ligaments in her left knee, and since she was still in considerable pain we did not ask her to show jump – the other three team members were in any case lying first, second and third, positions they still retained at close of play. Mary and King William nevertheless came out for the final parade in the main arena.

The following spring they led from start to finish at Badminton. Next came the Barcelona Olympics, and sadly this was where the big horse's problems in the showjumping phase of a three-day event first became apparent. On the previous day the amalgam of heat, humidity, flag-waving crowds and general excitement had most unexpectedly caused him to go right through his bit, and now he paid scant respect to the coloured poles, a failing which

has blighted his three-day event career ever since. Thus though his dressage has improved and improved, perhaps reaching a zenith at the Atlanta Olympics, showjumping has remained a nightmarish Achilles' heel, which even the dedication, iron nerve and brilliance of Mary has been unable to cure.

I will nevertheless always remember him with awe. Few horses can ever have combined such a commanding presence with such fluent paces, such boldness across country, and such a big, big heart.

Mary on King William

'It is an honour to be William's rider, and to have him in my yard. We form such a wonderful understanding and partnership – he's a really great friend and companion.

'I'm completely in his debt: his amazing soundness and consistency has kept my name at the top of the sport for so long, and he has taught me so much about cross-country riding through his natural talents of boldness, courage and speed. He gave me my first British team appearance at the Europeans at Punchestown in 1991, and my first title – British Open Champion – in the same year, plus one bronze and three gold medals.

'He has enabled me to fulfil my lifelong ambition of winning Badminton and competing at the Olympics – and if he were human David wouldn't have stood a chance!'

Left: Country Life's *portrait of Mary and William encapsulates the special bond between them*
Above: Mary's favourite trot-up photograph of William, taken at Badminton
Overleaf: William displays his athleticism at Gatcombe in 1995

LOVE AT

'My first impression on seeing William was "If he doesn't win Badminton no one will!"
Even as a five-year-old he looked so mature and had this amazing presence. Watching him
go cross-country is a very awesome experience as he seems to make everything look like a
Pony Club fence. He has such wonderful power and the ability to get out of tricky situations
– with a little help from Mary, of course!

'I think we all love William so much because he is so genuine and kind and, contrary to
everyone's opinion, is not a show-off. I always feel that it's more a question of
"Oh no, they're all looking at me". This has, of course, manifested itself in his showjumping
at the higher levels, where things go to pieces because of his nerves. I've seen him stand in
the collecting ring shaking with worry, but he still goes in and does his best. We all feel so
sorry for both him and Mary when we know how brilliantly he jumps at home and at the
one-day events.

'Whatever William does in the future is, as far as I'm concerned, a bonus –
Badminton was always the one I wanted Mary to win, so all the other successes were
icing on the cake. It has been such a privilege to be associated with such a wonderful
horse and I feel extremely proud that he has brought, and will continue to bring, so much
pleasure to so many people.'

Gill Robinson, co-owner

Pages 14–15: A leisurely hack in the picturesque surroundings of Salcombe Regis

FIRST SIGHT

'Wow! What a *fabulous* horse!'

Mary's immediate reaction on seeing William at the Alexanders' yard in the autumn of 1988 has been echoed by his many fans throughout the eventing world ever since. Her first sight was of a big bay horse with a great white blaze taking a good look at her over his top door, his bright alert expression eclipsing all the other horses in the yard. And when he was led out she was even more impressed: this beautiful horse, standing 16.3hh, with a high head carriage and tremendous presence even as a five-year-old, glossy bay in colour with wonderful dapples all over his body. It certainly was love at first sight…

So began one of the most successful partnerships the eventing world has ever seen: William, ⅞ TB by Nickel King, out of a ¾ TB mare, with his tall, aloof carriage and his immensely powerful physique has captured the hearts of young and old the world over; and Mary's skilful and sympathetic handling of this hugely strong yet surprisingly nervous horse has earned universal respect and admiration.

William's first three-day event was at Le Lion d'Angers in the autumn of 1989. One of the youngest horses ever to have taken part, he still looks a real baby (above); but tackled the cross-country like a champion (right)

BRUT -

SAUMUR

The early years

'I first heard about William through Geoff Orrock, a friend, who had been looking out for young horses for me. He rang to say that he'd seen a lovely horse at a local show, and that it was worth my going straight up to see him, which I did. He was called "Welcome" and was in Clive and (then) Bernice Alexanders' yard near Newbury. They'd bought him at a Warner, Sheppard and Wade sale at Stoneleigh, and had schooled him well on the flat and taken him to a few jumping shows. I was quite lucky, because Rodney Powell was apparently very interested in him; not wanting to tread on anyone's toes, I rang Rodney's yard and was told that he had just gone on holiday, and to go ahead – so I did!

'My first impression was of this huge, tall horse with a striking white face. He seemed to ooze power and energy; being only a youngster he was a bit like a gawky teenager, but you could see the power that he would develop as he matured. I fell for him straightaway! When he trotted up you were immediately struck by his enthusiastic, forward attitude, although actually his movement wasn't that wonderful; consolidated schooling on the flat has developed the elevation and brilliance of his paces.

'When I saw him ridden he moved with such grace and presence, and was consistently happy and enthusiastic, his ears pricked forwards all the time. Bernice jumped him over a small parallel, and he was a bit quick off the ground – too keen, really, and kept knocking out the front rail – maybe an omen?! – but then he jumped it well.

'When I got on him I wondered if I really wanted something so tall and powerful – and whether he would get too strong for me. But he was very comfortable, and when he jumped he never wavered – all he wanted to do was jump what was in front of him, and there was never any question of him running out or stopping.

'My main worry was the poor conformation of his legs – which is ironic, since he has proved to be just about the soundest horse on the eventing circuit; he has never missed a competition, or even a day's work! He is slightly tied in below his knee, and also slightly back at the knee; he is pigeon-toed, and has shallow heels in front, which if he were anything but well shod would spell real trouble; and although his hindlegs are powerful, both hocks have curbs. I asked Peter Scott-Dunn to vet him; he felt that these faults wouldn't stop him doing what I wanted, and so passed him.

'I couldn't believe that I'd bought such a fabulous horse! He was £8,000, which was about the average for a promising horse, and ownership was shared by Gill [Robinson] and David [King]. Right from the start William was special, maybe because he was so striking. When he came down off the lorry he seemed so tall – he held his head and neck really high as he looked around, and he would always do this at anything strange, seeming to grow until he was at least 18hh! I remember wondering if I was *ever* going to be able to control him!'

William rockets up the grades   William settled in quickly, and Mary thought she'd try one Novice event that autumn – Lulworth horse trials, in Dorset.

'I worked him a lot on the flat, trying to teach him to carry himself and not to pull my arms out – which he would do, even at trot! I wasn't worried about the jumping because he was so naturally bold; but I did wonder if I'd prepared him enough. But when I was working him in, he felt really good – and so naïve, in that he seemed perfectly content.

'He led after the dressage, and went across country as if he'd been doing it all his life! There was a tricky coffin, which was causing a lot of trouble, but he just cantered up to it and popped through – rail, ditch, rail – as if he'd done hundreds of them. I'd never taken him cross-country schooling as such; all he'd done was Bernice's bits and pieces in her field. Also he kept absolutely straight; young horses will generally wobble and spook a bit, and then rush off; but William has never, ever given me that feeling; when he's tense he tends to drift to the left as he jumps, but otherwise he's always jumped in a smooth, forward rhythm.'

The pair won at Lulworth, and the following spring, when William was six, he won or was placed at every Novice event he entered. He only made one mistake, at Crookham horse trials: 'We were cantering along and he was making it all feel incredibly easy, and maybe I was in rather a daze, but we approached a corner, and to my horror he just cantered past it!' Mary admitted that she hadn't 'set him up' for the fence at all, but had assumed that he would keep going straight and jump it – so it wasn't really his fault. He won his first Intermediate event at Ragley Hall, and so Mary determined that she would aim to take him to Le Lion d'Angers, a CCI 2* three-day event in France, that autumn. This is known to be an excellent first three-day competition for young horses, and although William would probably be amongst the youngest ever to have tackled it, Mary felt that it would be well within his capabilities.

'William was very alert throughout the journey – it was his first trip abroad; we took the ferry from Portsmouth to Caen, then drove on down to Le Lion d'Angers. He lost quite a bit of weight, and I remember thinking, "Oh dear, he does look a bit slim" – but he settled down to eat quite happily once we arrived.

'The venue for the event was the main stud for Percheron horses. Our stabling was on the end of the stable yard, and the track where these rather chubby, hairy horses trotted up and down with their carriages ran along "our" end – and William couldn't take his eyes off them! He spent most of the week with his head and neck bolt upright so that his ears were squashed down at an angle against the door lintel of his stable! What with these strange horses and carriages, and the stallions being led out every day, and him always being so alert anyway, I was afraid he'd be exhausted before the competition even started!

After his 6th place at Le Lion d'Angers, William continued to show what he was capable of: (top) at Portman horse trials in 1989; (above) at Belton in 1991; (right) as a seven-year-old at Blenheim in 1990

'But the event went pretty smoothly: William was still a comparative novice to do an FEI 2* dressage test, but even so, he was the best of the British and he finished in the top ten after the first phase; I knew he could still improve, but I was delighted with his test.

'On speed and endurance day he was an absolute dream: this was his first-ever steeple-chase, and I was consciously having to slow him down because he found the speed so easy. On the cross-country course I was determined not to chase for time; being such a young horse I wanted him to have a good, confidence-giving round – but he was superb! We had a few time penalties, which didn't worry me a bit because I knew the speed was there.

'We had just one fence down on the final day in the showjumping, which again I wasn't too worried about, and so he finished in 6th place. This gained him enough points to be upgraded to Advanced, which was a remarkable achievement for a six-year-old.'

Consolidation before big time competition
Mary's 1990 plan for William was initially to aim for the 3* three-day event at Bramham, in Yorkshire, in late spring. He started the year by competing in OI one-day events, and all went very smoothly, except at Belton: here he tipped up, but through no fault of his own. There was a new fence, a coffin which was sited under some trees with a slope down to the ditch, then a slope up to the rail out, and quite a few horses buckled on landing on the bank up – including William! No one is sure whether it was the lighting, or the footing, or what:

'Poor William had been cantering effortlessly round, and jumped in, and then jumped the ditch – and then just crumpled into the bank! It came as such a surprise to both of us, and when he picked himself up he had sand all over his white face! But he carried on as if nothing had happened at all, and this cool, confident attitude was really amazing for a young horse of his relative inexperience.

'William was one of the youngest horses at Bramham, although I was quite confident that I would not be overfacing him. My main worry wasn't the size of the fences but the distances involved – I didn't want to tire him so much that he risked making mistakes in his jumping. He was fairly well up after the dressage, and then across country we had a few time penalties because I was being careful – but this didn't worry me a bit, because I knew that speed would never be a problem. He moved up from 10th to 8th after the cross-country, and after jumping clear in the showjumping, moved up finally to 6th; this was really brilliant for a seven-year-old!

'There was another, equally successful, horse at Bramham that year: Robert Lemieux's Just An Ace. He and William have really tracked each other in the course of their careers since that Bramham in 1990.'

On track for William's first Badminton

'I took William to Blenheim in the autumn planning to aim him for Badminton in the spring – although he wasn't ready to do a 4* event that autumn, I felt that if he did well at Blenheim, and increasing in maturity all the time, Badminton would be perfectly feasible. His dressage was improving all the time as he was growing in strength and confidence, and learning about true engagement and self-carriage, and across country he had always felt wonderful. Sure enough at Blenheim he gave me a beautiful ride, in pretty bad conditions – it rained continuously and was really muddy – and we pulled up to 3rd or 4th. In the showjumping he had three fences down, and dropped to 9th. Little did I realise that this was the shape of things to come.'

But Mary was determined that William should attempt his first Badminton in 1991. In those days it was usual to do Burghley in the autumn and then Badminton, so when she took him to Blenheim, people were quite surprised about her Badminton plans, particularly as he was only eight. But she had complete confidence in his ability; she knew that she wouldn't be overfacing him '…because he wasn't that sort of horse'. She did four one-day events with him in preparation, and remembers that eventful Badminton very clearly:

'He did a lovely test, and was well up the leader board, and this was a great achievement because he was really quite immature. We were one of the first to go across country, and this was to play against us. In 1991 the course ran clockwise, so that Huntsman's Close was quite an early fence. William was going well, not pulling and perfectly relaxed; we jumped smoothly and quietly through Huntsman's Close, turned to find our line for the next fence, the Elephant Trap – and the next thing I knew we were flat on the ground! It was just such a surprise! It had rained, so it was a bit greasy on that turn, and it hadn't been appreciated how insecure the footing was; after William's fall, sand and grit was put down to improve the going.

'If we'd gone later he probably wouldn't have slipped. We were also given sixty penalties: in those days each fence carried a penalty zone, and a fall within its perimeter would automatically carry sixty penalties; because the two fences were quite close the penalty zones overlapped. Today the rules have changed, and we wouldn't have had faults. William was remarkable; he picked himself up and carried on round the course as if nothing had happened, with a composure that would have been impressive in an experienced horse.

'On the following day in the showjumping he had three down, just as at Blenheim. Obviously this was disappointing, yet I was still over the moon that he had coped so well – and the selectors were sufficiently impressed to put him on the longlist. To ride in the British team was one of my greatest ambitions; I had been shortlisted with King Boris, but had never been selected – and here in William I had a horse which would perhaps fulfil my dreams!'

'Mary and William striding out across country have brought a truly majestic flavour to many an event... especially at Badminton in 1992. Conditions were fatally treacherous... but King William never put a foot wrong... his lack of attention over the coloured poles on the final day was far more worrying for his many fans – perhaps it was this combination of invincibility across country and fallibility in the showjumping arena that helped make him so popular – but this time he kept the honours his cross-country brilliance had earned.'

Alan Smith
The Daily Telegraph

LIFE AS A

'It is always a great relief to discover that King William has been drawn in another division at any Advanced horse trial. With his normal dressage advantage, his more-often-than-not clear round showjumping, before his reliable fast cross-country, it usually means that the best the rest of us can hope for is second place. Actually, come to think of it, I much prefer it when Mary selects a different three-day event for William than one I have planned for my horses as well!'

Blyth Tait

SUPERSTAR

Having won his first event as a five-year-old, William has stayed at the top of the eventing ladder, and at fifteen has proved himself to be one of the most talented and sound horses in the history of horse trials. He hasn't missed a competition or even a day's work through lameness or ill-health, and always has enormous enthusiasm and style. Perhaps this is why so many make a special effort to watch him on event days, to admire his powerful, glossy body as he strides past the veterinary panel, his grace and elegance in the dressage, the ease with which he eats up any cross-country course.

His career achievements have been phenomenal. He has won 1,920 horse trials points – more than any other horse, ever. However, Mary's role in William's achievements should never be underestimated; with typical modesty she will describe a brilliant test or a faultless cross-country round as if all the credit is William's, and she is just a passenger! Although his temperament is far from straightforward, Mary never blames him when things go wrong, never gets cross with him, and if William is having problems, her immediate concern is what she can do to help him. As a result he trusts her implicitly, and so you feel will always do his best for her.

British Open Champions for the first time

After Badminton William was longlisted for the European Championships. Mary felt that if they were to have any chance of being picked for the team they would have to do something 'pretty special'. All the longlisted riders had to ride at Gatcombe, the final selection trial, and she knew that they had to jump a big, demanding course without a hiccup.

William led after the dressage, and then showjumped clear. Gatcombe is unique in that the cross-country is run in reverse order, making the whole day much more exciting because the competition builds to a real climax. But it does put much more pressure on the riders: Ian Stark was lying 2nd on Murphy, and Mary and William 1st, and Mary remembers how nervous she felt as they warmed up together for the cross-country.

'I was terribly aware of the extra pressure on us. I had awful butterflies, and I told Ian that I felt incredibly ill, and he said "Me too!" – but then I thought, "He can't be, he's on Murphy who's so experienced, and William's still a novice by comparison, and it's the first time he's really been in a position to dispute the lead" – and said as much; and Ian replied: "Mary, the older you get, the worse that feeling becomes!" And I thought, "But I can't feel worse than I do at the moment, perhaps I'd better give up now!"

'Then Ian set off, and shortly after so did I. There was only a point or two between us, and Murphy was so reliable cross-country I was half resigning myself to being 2nd or 3rd; though I hoped we'd still be chosen for the British team. But as we galloped along I heard on the loudspeaker that something had happened to Ian – normally you don't hear anything – and as I jumped the last fence and galloped up to the finish I was aware of the commentator again: "Is she inside the time? Has she got time faults? No, she hasn't: here is the new British Open Champion!" It was tremendously exciting, because not only were we defending Boris's title, but this was William's first real recognition in the sport.'

Riding for Britain – at last!

William and Mary were then invited to join the British team for the European Championships at Punchestown, Ireland. Mary and King Boris had been shortlisted for the World Games in Stockholm, and it had always been Mary's overriding ambition to ride for Britain on William.

'I'd always yearned to wear that little felt Union Jack on my jacket! Once on, it's there for life; I only stitched mine on at the last minute, after William had passed the vetting, because I didn't want to have to give it back! The other members were Ian Stark, Karen Dixon and Richard Walker, and Katie Meacham rode as an individual.

'It was interesting going for the first time with the team. The others had done it before,

William powers his way around the British Open Championship course at Gatcombe

Left and top: Team members at last! The European Championships at Punchestown were held in glorious sunshine, and the cross-country course – of imaginative design and beautifully built, and over the lovely old turf – was a joy to ride
Above: Mary, smartly dressed in the the team uniform, and William at the initial veterinary inspection

so I felt very much the newcomer, but I was conscious of a tremendous feeling of patriotism, excitement and camaraderie; I wasn't unduly nervous – just extremely proud! The team's support group was Lord Patrick Beresford, the chef d'équipe, and Paul Farringdon, the vet. We made a little British area in the stables – up went the Union Jack – and then the team went to stay in a hotel, which certainly helped to reinforce our team spirit.'

As the least experienced, Mary and William were third to go; generally the most experienced combination goes first to try and guarantee a fast clear, and on this occasion it was Richard Walker. At only eight years old, William was the real 'baby' at this relatively prestigious event.

'Ferdi Eilberg came out to help with our dressage. I remember William being very strong – at times he was so full of energy he was on the edge of exploding! In the judges' eyes he obviously showed enormous impulsion and flair, and we were in the lead individually after the dressage; the British team also led after the first two days. It was all very exciting!

'It was so different competing as a team member, walking the course together, discussing the fences, being advised by the more experienced riders. But it wasn't all serious: I remember we had time to kill after the dressage, and Ian persuaded all of us except Karen to go water-skiing. The selectors had forbidden this, but we sneaked off like a group of naughty schoolkids – and it nearly ended in disaster, too, when Katie almost crashed into a buoy: the boat went one side of it, and the buoy ended up going right between her legs! It was so funny; but the following morning – cross-country day – I was so stiff!

Ups and downs at Punchestown: (above) Gold medals all round; (right) A ducking at The Mill Pond

'The course was big and causing lots of problems, but William gave me the most fantastic ride. Then we came to the penultimate fence, the Mill Pond, where, as has been so well documented, he just buckled on landing in the water, and I was thrown off. I couldn't believe it – my first British team, and I had thrown away our chances! I was overwhelmed by a feeling of massive disappointment, of letting everyone down, and of despair at not being able to prove what William was really capable of. William very kindly trotted back and I was legged up again; then we had to jump back into the water to rejoin the course, and William tried to jump back up the huge drop! He would never have made it, but he was so naïvely bold that he actually took hold of the bridle and was gathering himself to try and jump back up this great wall – I remember shouting "No, William!", and hauling on one rein to bring him round.

'We fell because I hadn't really thought through the advice we were given by the selectors and the support group. Probably it would have been difficult to have gone against their advice, given that we were the 'novice' members, but in retrospect the way I approached it was wrong. Basically I was told to keep cantering towards the big drop in, because those who were coming in slowly were stopping. But William never stops – I should have trotted so that he had time to appreciate what a big drop it was, and was in better balance. He really just cantered over the edge – you can see from the photos that he didn't launch himself off at all. Nowadays how you tackle a fence is left much more to the individual.

'I'd hurt my knee, and it soon became very painful. William seemed relatively unscathed apart from a small cut on his knee which needed stitching. The other team members went brilliantly, and at the end of the day were still in the lead; but I was really sad to have blown our individual chances; that's the only time that William's has been the discard score.

'My knee was incredibly sore and swelling visibly, and x-rays showed that I had torn the ligaments; but with ice treatment I was able to hobble around. But next morning it was extremely painful. Ian trotted William up for me at the veterinary inspection, and William really looked magnificent, bounding along with his usual power and enthusiasm and not in the least sore or stiff; it just showed what an incredibly tough horse he is.

'When I got on William to showjump I knew immediately that it was hopeless, so I had

The ultimate victory: winning at Badminton!

Every inch a winner!

to withdraw, which was awful. The other three members jumped clear, so the team won the gold medal – but in a way I felt quite a fraud when it came to receiving our winners' trophies. When the others did their lap of honour, I crept away.'

Mary was sufficiently philosophical to put this disappointment behind her; backed by her many friends and supporters, and buoyed up by William's own ebullient temperament and good health, she was soon looking forward to the next challenge: Badminton 1992.

Crowning glory
Mary and Annie knew that William was as well prepared as possible for this enormous challenge, and that the selectors would be looking for possible British Olympic team members. Officially the event starts with the competitors' briefing on Wednesday morning, and Mary took William for a quiet hack first, having arrived at midday on the Tuesday. Competitors are always taken on a formal tour of the roads and tracks and steeplechase, though this usually becomes a mad race in the four-wheel-drive vehicles provided; the cross-country course is opened at midday on the Wednesday. 'The first course-walk gives you a general feel for the track, but I thought it looked very jumpable; it was similar to the year before when William had gone so well, which made me feel quite confident.'

In the afternoon William was polished and plaited for the first veterinary inspection; which takes place in front of Badminton House in the evening. William had been drawn no 38, and looked magnificent, his dappled bay coat gleaming, and his powerful trot raising a cheer from his admirers. Later Mary took him for a school: '…he went really well. Very often in a new place he gets really strong, but he seemed quite settled, and was soft and responsive.

'William's dressage test was on Thursday afternoon, and I was still worried that he might be too strong. I had to find just the right balance when working in, so that he was sufficiently contained to be obedient, but not so tired that he lost his enthusiasm and powerful forward movement.

'Early on Thursday morning we went for a good canter. I wanted him to have a good workout, but not to feel under any pressure. Annie took him for a bite of grass to keep him relaxed and happy, and later we had a schooling session with Ferdi. William went quite beautifully; I was beginning to feel really excited, and couldn't wait to start! I let him walk about quietly near the dressage collecting ring so he could get used to the applause and the general bustle, then took him back to the stables. I planned to get on him forty minutes before his test; it took about ten minutes to hack over to the practice arenas, and I wanted half an hour to work him in.

'Before his test he felt wonderful – calm, smooth and relaxed, yet still full of impulsion and energy. Ten minutes before the test I took him up to the collecting ring; when the previous competitor came out I kept him well back until the applause had died down. In the arena he perked up again quite a bit, but managed to contain himself and performed a very obedient and active test. His brightness showed in his lateral work because he was trying to tilt his head, and I didn't dare ride out his extended trot as much as I'd have liked because by then I felt he was on the brink of exploding!'

His performance obviously impressed the judges, however, and the pair took a good lead ahead of some very good combinations, including Ginny Leng and Master Craftsman; and they were still in 1st place by the end of Friday. On that day Mary gave William a good pipe-opener along Worcester Avenue, then walked him quietly back to the stables. By evening it was raining, and Mary woke several times to hear the rain falling in torrents; and in the morning it was no better.

'I got up at 6.30am because I like to walk the course one last time before there are too many people about. The lake fence was worrying me most, largely because of Punchestown – we couldn't afford another mistake over water if we were to catch the selectors' eye. It involved a jump in over some very big rails, then the direct route out was up a step with a bounce to a very narrow arrowhead. I decided to take the long route both in and out, and felt as if a huge weight had lifted from my shoulders – I could think about the rest of the course much more positively. The conditions were deep and slippery, and so I knew I should play safe.

'At last it was time to go! I bandaged William's legs – I always like to bandage the horses' legs myself – and then we were off! It was such a relief to get going – the spectators cheer and this really lifts your spirits, and William's easy trot covered the one kilometre per four minutes with no trouble. I could hear enough of the commentary to learn that Mark Todd had fallen and that the course was held, and I just prayed that William wouldn't get hurt – as he trotted along with his ears pricked, so enthusiastic and happy, I just felt how vulnerable he was, and how great was my responsibility in helping him to accomplish safely the task ahead.

'William is a wonderful horse to ride on the steeplechase because he has such a great rhythm and smooth, galloping jump. The going was getting really quite sticky, but he didn't seem to mind, and we finished well within the time.

'I let him walk the first kilometre of phase C to recover his breath, then we picked up the trot again. As you come over the hill on the last part of this phase you can see the crowds and hear the loudspeaker again, and I learned that Jane Holderness-Roddam had retired at the Vicarage Vee. She is very experienced, and it made me seriously wonder what was happening on the course, particularly when Mark Phillips greeted me with the news that only one horse had gone clear – and I was no 38! His last words were very good advice: "Go carefully, but be positive – and concentrate every step of the way." And then we were being counted down!

'I tried to ride William in a strong rhythm so he had enough impulsion to tackle the

Above: William gave an impressive performance, even though to Mary he felt explosive

Left: Looking good just before his test

Left: A trot-up with William is often a test of Mary's fitness, too!

jumps safely, but with enough control so as not to risk slipping on the turns and approaches. But he was finding it all easy and was just cruising along in fourth gear, and I didn't think about time at all, knowing that we had more speed if we needed it. He was loving every minute; he would land with his ears pricked, looking for the next jump, yet still remaining responsive and obedient to my aids. He did a huge jump over the oxer before Fairbanks, and I steadied him and he came into my hand straightaway, so we took the direct route over the Fairbanks Drop with no trouble.

'Down the Beaufort Staircase he drifted slightly left, but I needed only to lead him slightly right-handed to take the final element. As we approached the Mitsubishi Corners William was again most helpful and sensible because we were catching up another competitor and he had to steady quite rapidly. This was a big double of corners, the last of the real "problem" fences, and at this stage he might well have been tiring and becoming heavy in my hand, particularly with the deep going; but he felt just as strong, and jumped with as much athleticism as if he'd only just set out! My heart went out to him for his generous, enthusiastic attitude, and in true admiration for his seemingly bottomless stamina and energy. When I urged him to go a bit faster he surged forwards with his ears pricked; yet he obediently steadied for the Ha Ha and for the Stick Pile.

'As we landed over the last I was suddenly aware of the crowd shouting, "Come on, William!", and it was with a tremendous feeling of elation that we galloped through the finish. I circled him quietly to stop him, and then suddenly there seemed to be hundreds of people crowding round. I was so thrilled at his marvellous performance that I chattered away incoherently; then a message came from Annie to say he had a cut on his pastern which might need stitching, and my elation suddenly evaporated in my concern that he was all right. Stitching would make him sore, and I desperately wanted him to showjump the following day to prove what a brilliant horse he was. Eventually he had three stitches, which he didn't seem to notice, and laser treatment to help reduce the pain.

'The following morning he was slightly unlevel when we trotted him up, so we put some ice just above the cut to help reduce the heat and swelling, then left him to finish his breakfast. About an hour before the final veterinary inspection I took him for a quiet hack in the park, and his stride soon felt free and loose. And at the trot-up he was most impressive: everyone cheered him, and he was sure that all these people had come just to look at him!

'Once again I could feel only gratitude and admiration towards him: most horses would have felt pretty sorry for themselves with a cut like that, and certainly leg-weary – but not William! As he bounded past the Ground Jury, he proved beyond all doubt that he is a horse of incredible toughness and indomitable courage: a true star!'

On the final day of the event the sun shone. The Parade of Competitors was at 2pm, and then the top twenty combinations showjumped in reverse order of merit. It was particularly important for Mary to remain calm and relaxed with William who could so easily become tense; then he was inclined to rush at the fences and hollow his neck and back, and so risked knocking them down.

'As I warmed up, Stephen Hadley and Captain Mark Phillips both came and helped me, which was really reassuring because William wasn't being particularly careful over the practice fences. He produced one good jump shortly before we were due to go in, so we left it at that – any more and we might have worried him and so spoiled what we had. Ginny had gone clear, so we had just one fence in hand – and actually the pressure was enormous, though I didn't dare let myself think about it, because the year before he had had three fences down.

Elated and happy, Mary weighs in after William's brilliant cross-country round

'Then it was our turn! William had a major spook at the fountain as we came in, and I concentrated on establishing a short, engaged canter; but he still hit the first fence quite hard. He was worrying about the crowds, the flashing cameras and that frightening fountain, and I had to make a conscious effort to keep relaxed and my hand soft – if I was at all sharp, he would probably throw up his head even more. He seemed to rattle every fence, causing frequent oohs and aahs from the spectators, which didn't help his concentration. And then he had the first part of the final double down, but he made a special effort over the final part and there was a roar from the crowd – we'd done it! We had won Badminton, my greatest ambition, and one of the highest achievements for any event horse!

'I could hardly think straight, and when we went back into the arena for the prize-giving I still just couldn't believe we had really won, even when we were presented with the wonderful trophy! The crowd gave William a rousing reception during his lap of honour, and then there were endless photo calls and press conferences.

'I loved all of it, but we now know that it really upset William. When Annie took him back to the stables he was quite unsettled, pacing round his box and snatching at his hay, standing with his head really high, his body quivering. On the way home he became increasingly

'We've done it!' William proves his remarkable cross-country ability in truly appalling conditions

uneasy, weaving and staring round wildly, and Annie was seriously worried that he was developing colic; I travelled back in the lorry with him, and found that the only way to calm him down was to rub up and down the top of his neck the whole way home. By the time we got there he seemed almost back to normal. Because of all the excitement he became abnormally wound up, and suffered clinical stress. Most horses generally learn to cope, but he was never able to settle down at a major three-day event again. But none of this was obvious at the time, and once we were safely home and he was settled happily in his own box, the true significance of our achievement began to really sink in: we had *won* Badminton!'

Lead-up to Barcelona So William was shortlisted for the Olympic team. His preparation for the Games was worked out in meticulous detail, starting straight after Badminton. He was allowed seventeen days holiday (only then does a horse at rest start to lose muscle bulk), and then brought quietly back into work. Mary was helped in her showjumping and dressage preparation by Stephen Hadley and Ferdi Eilberg:

'We just had to produce a good performance at the final trial at Savernake Forest horse trials at the beginning of July. In the showjumping I had to keep him as soft and round in his canter as possible so that he could use himself properly over a jump. Steve felt that I needed to increase the pressure I could feel in my hand so that William was really contained between hand and leg on the approach – otherwise he tends to launch himself forwards over a fence without having first got high enough in the air.

'Ferdi advised me how to put even more expression and lift into William's paces. When I asked for more William directed all his energy forwards and became very strong. So we worked on downward transitions from extended to collected canter to encourage him to use the engagement of his quarters, and not my hand, to steady himself; he had to learn to put his energy into lifting his stride rather than into lengthening it and speeding it up, so it was contained within the working pace.'

A week before the final trial Mary took William to Doddington Park horse trials. 'I wanted to see how he reacted to the competition atmosphere, and expected him to be quite onward-bound; but he surprised me by being very relaxed and well behaved, and did a super test. His showjumping really pleased me because he stayed much straighter, and didn't rush – he jumps best when I can ride him forwards into each fence rather than having to slow him down all the time. This made me much more confident about the final trial.'

In fact William was tense in the dressage at Savernake, and reverted to his old habits in the showjumping and had two fences down. Mary took him very quietly across country – '…it did feel strange going so slowly' – knowing that he had only to go clear and finish sound to be selected. The fifteen longlisted horses went back to Badminton house that night; the team would be announced after the final trot-up the following morning.

'Although I half knew we would be chosen, it was a great thrill to hear my name called out, along with Ginny Leng, Ian Stark and Richard Walker; Karen Dixon was travelling reserve. The selected horses and the reserves had one final fastwork trial at Lambourn at the end of the week, and they all passed the trot-up the next day. Then the four non-travelling reserves went home, and the five team members moved into Badminton.'

Training the nominated riders at Badminton fosters a strong feeling of team spirit; it distances them from any domestic worries, and also the press. They have their own rooms above the stables, and are thoroughly pampered. Ferdi was the official dressage trainer, but riders were allowed their own trainers, and so Steve and the Captain were able to help Mary. She was anxious not to pressurise William too much:

'I only jumped William a couple of times during the eleven days we were there, and I had just two or three lessons with Ferdi. Every four days the horses were boxed up and taken to Lambourn to be galloped, which was great fun! There were press days, and there was an

A steady build-up for William and Mary in 1992: (overleaf) at Brigstock, and at the final trial at Savernake; (below) Olympic team training at Badminton

Open Day, when the public could watch us training and ask whatever questions they liked. One of the most exciting occasions was when we were given all our new equipment and clothing from the team sponsors – you'd never believe how tiring it is, scrambling in and out of one outfit after another! I was more exhausted after that day than any of the others!

'On the Thursday before we were due to fly out a Pedens lorry arrived and was loaded with all the spare tack and equipment. We galloped the horses at Lambourn again, and – maybe this was an omen – sadly Master Craftsman trotted out lame the following day. On Sunday the team horses had their final fastwork, and on the Monday the lorry came to pick them up: things were getting really exciting! William hadn't flown before, and I was a bit concerned about him, but all went well – he wasn't given his morning hay until he was on the plane, and munched happily throughout the two-hour flight.

'And all I could think was, "Barcelona, here we come!"'

Olympic ups and downs 'We flew out from Heathrow kitted out in

our Olympic outfits, and it was amazing – the plane was full of Olympic athletes, so you really felt part of the British squad. When we arrived we were taken to the Olympic compound where our living quarters were brand-new apartments, and there was a gargantuan food hall, with every type of food or drink, whenever you wanted it, all for free! One of the best things about it was you kept bumping into really famous people – you'd be sitting next to Linford Christie one day and Sally Gunnell the next!'

The three-day event took place at El Montanya, a fifty-minute drive from the Olympic village in the mountains north of Barcelona. The horses were stabled on site, and the grooms lived in hotels nearby.

'We could hack about in the area where phases A and C would take place, and there were showjumping and dressage arenas for schooling. I wanted William to have as relaxing a time as possible, so just worked him quietly, letting him get used to the atmosphere and humidity.

'The official briefing seemed to take forever, because everything had to be repeated in all the different languages. Then at last came the course-walk, which was a pleasant surprise: in El Montanya everything was hot, dusty and shrivelled, but the course wandered its way round a golf course and had a good covering of grass. The fences were pretty big, but there were plenty of alternatives and it all seemed quite jumpable; I was really excited at the prospect of tackling it, especially after our Rolls-Royce ride at Badminton.'

William had seemed to settle into his Olympic surroundings well. The day before the dressage phase competitors were allowed half an hour to work their horses in the main arena, and Mary looked forward to getting William used to the competition surroundings – but

'William started off by working well; but then the organisers tested the huge electronic score-board alongside the arena, and it made all these whirring, clicking noises – and this really upset William. He pranced about and snorted, and absolutely refused to go anywhere near it, and even when I took him right over to the other side kept looking over his shoulder, completely mesmerised by it. Our time was up before he was anywhere near settled.

'At the veterinary inspection William was very impressive and strong, towing me past the ground jury; I always imagined he was showing off to his fans, but in retrospect perhaps he was nervous of them pressing round his "space" and was trying to run away. The team was to go fourth, and I was the third rider, no 48; my dressage test was at 6.35pm on Monday evening, which was good news because by then it might be quieter and cooler.'

Mary determined to give William plenty of work before his test. She hacked him out in the early morning, then had a short showjumping school with Steve Hadley when William jumped '…better than I've ever known him do before, which left us feeling very excited!' She then cantered him a couple of times round the fastwork area. In the afternoon they had an intensive lesson with Ferdi, when '…although he worked well, he was becoming increasingly strong'; by this time he'd had four hours work, and when Mary got on him again half an hour before the test 'William settled down well in the practice arenas, but as soon as we reached the main arena he became tense and nervous. There were still huge numbers of people milling about, flags were waving, and of course the British supporters gave him a great cheer when he appeared; the whole atmosphere was highly charged. The Spanish crowd was very enthusiastic and noisy, too – whereas at any major British three-day event everyone is quiet until your test is finished, here they were cheering and clapping, and shouting "Good luck, Mary!" as we came in, and even during the test itself! This didn't help William, who was excited and tight to start with, and became stronger and more tense all the time. Considering how keyed up he was, he did a reasonable test, but his tension meant I couldn't ride out the movements as much as I'd have liked. But the others did really well, and at the end of the dressage phase the team was lying 1st, and individually Ian was 2nd, Karen 3rd and William and I were 4th!

'William was just hacked out quietly on Friday, and I walked the steeplechase and cross-country courses again that evening; usually I do this early on cross-country day, but because of the heat and humidity I decided I should conserve all my energy for the next day – little did I realise how right I was!'

On cross-country day William and Mary's start-time was nearer midday, so Mary watched the steeplechase for a while, and then saw the first ten riders on closed-circuit television, including Richard Walker's desperately unlucky stop and fall. She helped Annie get William ready – and then at last it was time to be off!

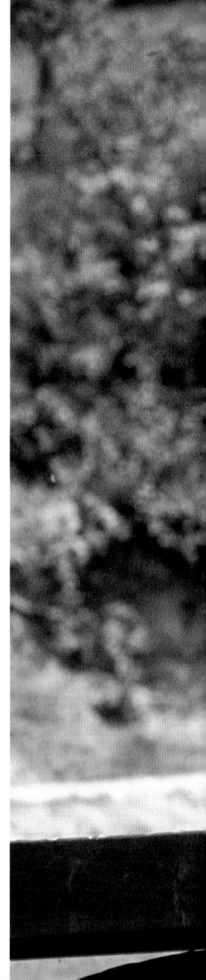

'After so many competitions at the highest level it is a great attribute
that he remains one of the toughest and soundest horses I have had
any responsibility for in ten years as an international event team
veterinarian. William could always be relied upon to finish the
toughest competition as sound as he started. This is a remarkable
achievement and a great compliment to his soundness and stamina
and to his management and training by Mary and her staff.'

John Killingbeck
British team vet at the Barcelona Olympics

Downhill all the way

'William felt really good on phase A, relaxed but bright; I rode carefully to avoid the rougher, stonier parts of the track, and kept in the shade where possible. There was quite a crowd of people watching the steeplechase, and as soon as he saw them his eyes went out on stalks and he shot up his head and neck like a giraffe; although he jumped the first few fences keenly, he was becoming increasingly strong in my hand – after each jump he would try and accelerate away, and I had very little control. He roared through the finish and I had to really fight to bring him back to a halt; for the first time ever he was completely ignoring the vulcanite pelham bit that he'd always performed so well in. He seemed to settle down again on phase C, however, and my feelings of alarm subsided.

'Jane Holderness-Roddam briefed me in the ten-minute box; I told her that I planned to take all the direct routes except at the Owl Holes, which the selectors thought was of dangerous construction, and possibly the last water complex if I felt William was tired. Karen had produced a good clear, and the course seemed to be riding well; so I set off full of confidence.

'William jumped the first fence in fine style, but as we galloped to the second he was becoming horribly strong. The crowds were wildly enthusiastic, shouting, cheering and waving – even booing those competitors who took a long route – and William seemed very nervous of them, almost as if he were trying to bolt away from them. The first five fences weren't very big and he just got faster and faster, and was increasingly jumping horribly flat. I managed to get him back enough to attempt the direct route at the farmyard complex, but he was accelerating alarmingly all the way through it; whilst I was just able to hold him on the approach to a fence, as soon as I released the rein to allow him to jump, he bolted off. The next combination was the first water complex, and I realised it wouldn't be safe to attempt the direct route; I just wasn't in control, and we would risk a nasty fall.

'We ended up going the long way at all the water complexes; all the way round people were shouting, "Well done, Mary! Go on, Mary!" – but this only frightened William even more, and as he got stronger and stronger, I became weaker and weaker. He completely ignored the pelham, and me on the end of it – his mouth was probably numb from pulling – and I was thinking "This is terrible, it's not 'well done' at all!"

'I've never been so pleased to see the finish of a course, and I've never ever experienced such an alarming ride. I was delighted to have gone clear, although taking the long routes was costly in time penalties, but otherwise I felt absolutely exhausted and utterly deflated. At the finish William looked as if he was ready to go round again, but I felt really sick and dizzy.

'Later we cleaned up and poulticed William's little cuts and grazes and put Ice-Tight on his legs; it was important that he trotted up the next day without any sign of undue stiffness or unlevelness. Otherwise he seemed quite unaffected by his irrational behaviour – which is more than can be said for me; I ached from head to toe, even after a relaxing swim.

'The team was now lying 2nd, Ian and Murphy having produced a brilliant round. But the following morning Murphy was lame, and after half an hour's walk which was meant to work off any stiffness, it was obvious that he wasn't improving as we'd hoped. Having been quite optimistic just a short while before, it was quite a shock to realise our chances of a medal were fast disappearing.'

Murphy failed the final veterinary inspection, and so the team was down to three. Mary's main concern was whether she would ever be able to hold William if he behaved as he had the day before. 'Scotty [Ian Stark] lent me a bucketful of bits, and I hacked William out at midday intending to try out some of them. However, he felt very soft and light, so I decided to keep him in his normal vulcanite pelham – sometimes a horse will react badly in the ring to a bit he isn't used to.

'Remarkably I didn't feel worried at all as our turn approached. Everything seemed to be conspiring against us: we all knew that showjumping wasn't William's strong point; after his wild, irrational behaviour the day before, I didn't have any idea how strong he would be; and having walked the course, it was obviously not going to suit the less careful horses – the jumps were all the same bland blue colour, with very few fillers to encourage the horses into the air. Worse, William was jumping very much to the left over the practice fences, which was always a sign of nerves and tension with him. So I wasn't expecting things to go well, and felt quite calm.

'In the showjumping arena there was very little to encourage him to concentrate; the spectators cheered and clapped during each round as well as after it, and I knew perfectly well that William's mind was simply not on the job. All I can say is we had five showjumps down; he was very tense because of all the noise and the highly charged atmosphere, and although he didn't get strong like the day before his canter was too flat and free, and I just couldn't get him to relax enough to stay round in his canter and lift his shoulders.

'In spite of this disappointment, I was still pleased with him: we had got to the Olympics, we had completed, and we were 9th in the world!'

Mixed fortunes in 1993

At Badminton William and Mary had five showjumps down and, effectively, were dropped from the team. William went some way to redeeming his reputation by winning the first Ford Maverick Championships at Althorp in July. In the autumn Mary had every intention of winning Burghley, '…just to show them all!' But William cut his pastern before performing a really beautiful dressage test to take the lead. The cut was stapled, but although the vet was happy he should run, the ground jury forbade them to continue… 'I was utterly shocked! My big mistake had been to mention the cut to the press,

As William became increasingly strong, Mary had to resort to swinging him from one side of the track to the other in an attempt to regain some sort of control

and the ground jury felt that if William's leg were to start bleeding the inevitable publicity would be bad for the sport. But I would never dream of running any horse if I didn't think it was fit; I was so stunned, and David was furious – but we just had to pack our bags and go home…'

A month later William and Star Appeal were entered for Boekelo; but the day before Mary had a phone call to say that Boekelo was cancelled because of torrential rain!

Triumph at the Hague

The long-term objective for William in 1994 was the World Equestrian Games in the Hague in July. Although at Badminton he had four fences down, he was long listed! Mary was hopeful that he would do well at the final trial at Althorp.

'William went really well to finish 6th, and the selectors wanted him! The previous year the European Championships at Achselschwang had been a disaster: the going was very deep and the team hadn't completed, and I think this made them realise how valuable William was, because he was remarkably tough and sound, and I'm sure he would have "come through".'

Mary was thrilled to be selected – and remembers with a smile: 'Our team kit included a long, narrow skirt with a small slit up the side, linen, quite fashionable but highly impractical for trotting up a powerful, big-striding horse! Anyway, there I was, mincing along, and

Winning at Althorp in 1993; the final trial for the World Equestrian Games in 1994 was also at Althorp

Badminton 1994: coming off the Fairbanks Drop in impeccable style

there was a loud tearing noise and the skirt split, right up to my crotch! William could've been quite lame, but the ground jury were so busy looking at my legs they wouldn't have noticed!

'William and I went first for the team, which suited him: his test would be early when it was quieter, and we knew he'd give the team a good start across country. But William had some serious problems: the cross-country was on a different site two hours' away, and he didn't settle well in the new stabling, sweating quite heavily, as he had on the journey. He was actually becoming increasingly dehydrated; also the roads and tracks phases were in deep, sandy going, and it was hot and humid.

'The first half of the course was twisty, and I wanted to catch up on time on the homeward part. So after the last water I asked for more speed – and he didn't respond at all! He seemed to be really struggling, so I determined to "nurse" him home, but pull up if he got any worse. To William's eternal credit he plugged on – he's so generous – but when we finished he made straight for a bucket of water, and it was only then that we realised how dehydrated he was.

'By showjumping day the British team was in gold medal position. We had five showjumps in hand, and I made it quite clear to the others that these were all ours! Obviously they didn't

Mary and William were part of the 1984 gold-medal winning team at the World Equestrian Games in the Hague. But it wasn't all plain sailing for William as the picture above demonstrates. He started to show signs of dehydration and had to dig deep into his reserves of stamina and resilience to finish the course

Right: A stunning portrait of William, taken during the showjumping phase. which shows what a powerhouse of a horse he is

listen because they used up three, and when William took out two parts of the treble my heart sank; but he cleared the rest, and the gold was ours! I was just so relieved that we hadn't let anybody down – and that William was quite unaffected by the rigours of the previous day.'

Pratoni's best-kept secret

At Badminton in 1995 William was unsettled even in the dressage. He'd never repeated his 1992 performance, and Mary was beginning to think she shouldn't bring him again. She also wondered how his low placing would affect his chances of being selected for the Open European Championships in Italy in the autumn. However, there was still the final team trial at Thirlestane – though Mary had other things to worry about, because she was pregnant! And she might not have got to either competition, because at Gatcombe, William made an uncharacteristic mistake:

'We were having a great round, and approaching a brush parallel. The next fence was away to the left, and whether I asked him to turn too soon, or he anticipated, he jumped violently to the left and collided with the wing, sending me and Emily rolling off down the hill! We were fine, but I played safe and retired!

'Thirlestane was good, with William 1st and Apple 2nd. Apple was lame afterwards, which left the selectors in a quandary because they'd wanted him for the team! Half the selectors didn't want William, but Bridget Parker, one of his long-time supporters, managed to persuade them.

'I wanted to keep my pregnancy a secret until I had finished competing, because if anything untoward happened the press would go berserk; so I asked the team doctor, who was also a gynaecologist, what I should do; he gulped, then advised me not to tell the selectors, but to go ahead as long as I felt well and happy – which I did! So at team training I took just William, and otherwise had a quiet week.'

Mary was the most experienced team member at Pratoni, having been there with King Samuel in 1992. This time certain aspects of the competition were more awkward than usual:

'The weather was warm, and I found course-walking quite hard work; uphill I would get left behind, and the others teased me. We'd travelled out in convoy, and our lorry was the slowest – it always lagged behind uphill – and I remember William Fox-Pitt saying, "You're a bit like your lorry!". Luckily the trot-up outfit had a loose jacket, because I had to let out the buttons on the skirt quite a lot! The press were most complimentary about it, making remarks like how slim I looked in it. I avoided the physiotherapist, too – she was a great one for massage, and with my bulging tummy I didn't want to strip off!

'My next worry was wearing my tailcoat for the dressage, because it stops short at the waist

William took Mary (and Emily!) safely round the cross-country at Pratoni

Team gold and individual bronze at Pratoni
1995. William and Mary win their very own,
highly deserved, medal

Top: Powering around the course at Pratoni

Far right: Up the Beaufort Staircase at
Badminton in 1995

and I felt really would show the bulge – Annie got fed up with me asking "Does it look all right? Are you sure?" I put it on at the last minute, and as soon as I had dismounted after my test I pulled it off quickly, and pulled my shirt out of my breeches saying something like, "Phew! Isn't it hot?!"

'William was number one again, and he was only just pipped at the post by Lucy Thompson and Welton Romance. On cross-country day he gave me a wonderful ride, which was such a relief! I remember thinking in the start-box, "Please William, look after me and my baby" – and he did! On the last day the team was leading, and we had three fences in hand. It was a big, open ring with no grandstands, but there was a treble on the side of the ring close to the spectators and flags, and I thought this might unnerve him; sure enough, he ran on here and had two down. But the final result was the team won gold, and Willam individual bronze.

'At last I could tell everyone my secret: Gill Robinson first, as our most loyal friend and supporter; and then Bridget Parker, chairman of the selectors, who exclaimed "Thank goodness you didn't tell me before the competition!" David then took me on holiday, as the horses also had theirs; that was the only way he could think of to stop me riding!'

Lead-up to Atlanta Mary had serious doubts about competing William at Badminton, but she had to if she wanted to be considered for a place in the Olympic team. However, she was determined that if he didn't go well she wouldn't take him again.

'He was more nervous than ever in the dressage, and if it hadn't been for the Olympics I would have pulled him out; he needs a really good lead in the dressage so we have a fence or two in hand on the last day. He did a fast clear across country and pulled up to 4th. However, we'll never know where William might have finished, because at the first cross-country fence Apple and I had a crashing fall. The next day I was very stiff, and the physiotherapist insisted I had my neck x-rayed, and sure enough there was a definite shadow which looked like a break. I was put in a neck brace and told not to move – and then had to wait for the specialist who was at home.

'Time was ticking on towards William's showjumping round, so David rang Bridget who told us not to hurry back because William was wanted for the team. A further x-ray reassured everyone that nothing was damaged.

'Having won Badminton, Olympic gold was now my ultimate goal. All those proposed for the Atlanta team had to have one last run at Hartpury College; this was a "closed" event, and wasn't meant to be ridden competitively. The showjumping was intentionally big, but William had only one down and finished third. So for a second time I could say, "Olympics, here we come!" '

A sigh of relief for the rider as the pair successfully negotiate The Lake at Badminton in 1996. This was the last time Mary ever took William to this event

On duty and off at the Atlanta Olympics in 1996
Top: William's dressage test was the best ever to have been performed at a 4* competition
Above: An informal portrait of Mary and William relaxing at Pinetops
Right: Eating up the cross-country course

Atlanta 1996

The British horses travelled out to Atlanta eleven days before the competition so they could acclimatise; the boxes in the Horse Park were cool and airy, and they settled in quickly. To Mary's genuine surprise she was to compete as an individual – she was relieved to know that the team's fate would not depend on William's showjumping! The team competition ran first, and Mary considered that '…it was certainly an advantage to watch the team going round the cross-country to see how they coped with the terrain.

'William was drawn early for his dressage, and worked in really well. He felt much more relaxed and responsive than he had been at a championship competition for ages. He was soft and obedient, and allowed me to ride him forwards so that I could help him perform with as much expression and flair as possible. I began to feel that his performance was as good as any I'd ever known him produce, and as we left the arena the crowd applauded wildly – they obviously thought it was something special, too!

Bathtime at Atlanta with William looking a little unsure

'Each judge gave us four nines for various movements, one gave us 191 marks – and I had nines for my riding! William's test was the best ever to have been performed at a 4* competition, and his score of 31.6 put him well into the lead. Annie was crying her eyes out, she was so proud of our "Willie" – and although I knew he was just as likely to throw away his advantage on the last day, on this occasion I couldn't have asked for more.'

Mary knew that the cross-country course wasn't particularly big or difficult for William, but it was twisty and undulating, and many of the turns had awkward cambers; several of the team horses fell on the flat. Mary's other concern was the heat and humidity, but the horses were continually monitored, and the climate was less hostile than was anticipated.

'At last we were off on phase D, with William feeling very smooth and focused. Now he's older he isn't so extravagant, but just does what he has to. About a third of the way round the course was a Helsinki steps-type fence, then a narrow treble of logs on a one-stride distance in an awkward dip into some woods; he jumped to the left, and I probably over-corrected him – suddenly we were on a bad stride to the first part of the treble. We scrambled over the first two elements, but then were too far to the right, and with very little impulsion left, and William ground to a halt. In his younger days he would probably have tried to jump it.

'It was such a terrible disappointment – when I thought of all the huge fences William had tackled in his career, and all the difficult combination fences, to have a silly stop at a relatively undemanding fence – when William never stopped – seemed just desperately unlucky. This was William's last chance at an Olympics, and we'd blown it. And of course William bowled merrily round the rest of the course; at the end of the day we finished in 7th place.'

On showjumping day Mary had a very tense William on her hands; he'd even been keyed up and jumpy at the veterinary inspection: 'His supporters gave him a tremendous reception – but people staring at him, and clapping and shouting, scares the daylights out of him! He might look as if he's loving it, but it's actually making him really apprehensive and nervous.

'He was definitely scared of the main arena. I think on the first day he hadn't worked out where he was, until the applause – and now that was all he could remember, and he felt as taut as a bowstring. He made a lovely round shape over the first fence, and my hopes rose; but as we turned for the second he noticed a group of photographers and tensed up, and he just ran at the fence and knocked it for six. Whatever I did – whether I tried to hold him off the fence, or softened my hand to him, he took it out – I can hardly believe we had eight down. By then I was beyond tears. It's just so sad that he can cope at a World and a European championships, but we just don't seem able to bring off an Olympics.'

British Open Champions again! At home again William looked a picture of health, and Mary decided to take him to Gatcombe at the end of August to defend his Open Championships title.

'The problem was that William was only just back from a major event and usually event horses finish their season after their autumn three-day. But the Olympics had been held early, and it was a long time for him to do nothing until the following year. I didn't want anyone to think I was over-using him, but the selectors said that if he looked fit and well, to go ahead: "As long as you're successful, that's fine! If you do badly, people will complain and say you're greedy, and you'll have a bad press – but if you do well, that's OK!" So I risked it, and he won! He only had one showjump down, and cruised round the cross-country, loving every minute of it. We'd come back from the Olympics flat and depressed, and for me and all William's supporters this was just wonderful; it really lifted our spirits!'

William winds down (but only a little!) In 1997 Mary remained true to her decision not to take William to Badminton: he had competed there every year since he was seven years old, and he was now fourteen.

'I had the younger horses, Star Appeal and King Solomon, and I wanted William to be

*Inset: Chantilly, 1997
William had the best dressage
and maintained his lead over
the three days to win*

*Far left: Cruising around the
cross-country at Gatcombe in
1996 to win the Open
Championship*

75

relieved of the pressure of three-day events. In the spring he did several one-day events: I didn't have to "save" him for the bigger championship events, so we could have a thoroughly "fun" time – and I am more relaxed at one-day events, too. I was aiming him for Punchestown, as a less prestigious three-day event than Badminton or Burghley, and one where he would feel less pressured. In fact he was so quiet that his dressage marks weren't as good as usual because he was less impressive! In the showjumping he had just two down, and ended up 6th.

'I'd also decided to take him to Chantilly, a 2* CIC competition similar to Gatcombe but run over three days; so there were no roads and tracks, and no steeplechase, and phase D was only eight-minutes. I was quite surprised at how competitive it was – all the New Zealanders were there with their top horses. William did a lovely dressage which put him in the lead, but he was quite tight and nervous in the showjumping and he had one down; he did maintain his lead, however. The cross-country was run in reverse order of merit, so William and I had to wait all day. It was a very tricky course, and there were a lot of problems. I remember watching the closed-circuit television and seeing all these riders falling off and horses stopping; it was well within William's capability but very twisty, the sort of course where you might easily make a silly mistake. William gave me a super ride, though had to fly round the last part to catch up on time; we had a couple of time penalties, but it was good enough to win. William had a really good time, the fences weren't too massive, and we all enjoyed it.

'That autumn I decided to aim him for Blenheim. Again we went in a relaxed frame of mind with no greater objective than to have an enjoyable three days. He performed a quiet, accurate test; he was really good on the cross-country; and had just two down in the showjumping. This was good enough for him to finish 3rd. So it was another thoroughly pleasurable event, not pushing him to the limit, but just keeping him feeling well, happy and fulfilled.'

William's Punchestown and Blenheim placings contributed towards a personal triumph when Mary finished 1997 as leading lady rider and number two in the world rankings after Blyth Tait, her three top horses having done consistently well in their three-day events.

'In 1998 the plan was to aim William for Bramham three-day event. We had great fun going round the spring one-day events – he ran in seven, and finished in the top three in all of them – and so set off for Bramham full of hope and enthusiasm (as always!). The last time William had gone to Bramham was as a seven-year-old when he had come 6th, so we were all wondering if he could come back as a fifteen-year-old and better his own result!

'But, similar to Atlanta, we fell victim to a silly hiccup: early in the course there were two elements with a sharp left turn to the second; whether William sensed I wanted him to go left, or maybe I actually indicated this to him, I don't know – but as he jumped the first part he swerved violently to the left and my leg caught the wing of the fence and was swept right up and over his quarters. I didn't actually fall off, but by the time I'd reorganised myself and was back in the saddle, we had passed the second part. Feeling really disappointed, I decided to retire; I felt I'd let him down by not anticipating that he might swing left too soon. The only mistakes he has made throughout his career have been as a result of his jumping to the left if I gave him the opportunity. In this case I could have asked him to jump the first element absolutely straight, and then turned him to the second, and he would've managed this perfectly well.

'Perhaps at any other time I would have continued, but on this occasion I have to admit to feeling considerably relieved that I hadn't fallen off, because William was once again carrying not only me, but another Emily!'

Below, Savernake and overleaf Bicton in 1998: William ran in seven one-day events in the spring, and was in the top three in all of them!

FAMILY, FANS

'It has been a privilege to have worked with such a great horse with such an unbelievable record. He has stirred the emotions of his many admirers when his nerves have got the better of him at critical moments. Equally Mary's ability to cope with the different sides of his character is unique: a lesson to all who experience the ups and downs which are inevitable in our sport.

'Many would have wanted to overcome his showjumping "problem" in a ruthless way – but Mary knew better. This proud and majestic horse would, in my view, not have responded to harsh methods. In spite of his proven courage when going cross-country, he is very sensitive and I feel that his nerves would take a long time to be repaired should the rider or trainer upset him. Everyone knows that the big occasion affects him, and he focuses on what happens around the fences rather than on the fences themselves. If, at those moments, the rider takes hold of him too much, this proud, strong horse becomes like a bull in a china shop. On the other hand, if one overdoes the silk glove approach he floats along and plays football with the poles.

'His natural high carriage and courage impress the dressage fraternity, but in jumping terms, he is not naturally engaged. Put the pressure on him in a tense situation and he finds it difficult to cope mentally and physically.

'His courage, which has made him such a great cross-country horse stays with him in the showjumping ring where we know a degree of caution is the order of the day. My feelings are that he is an unbelievable horse, but even more so that Mary is an unbelievable rider. If ever there was a situation which merited the Kipling poem: "If you can keep your head when..."'

Lars Sederholm

& FRIENDS

When Mary returned home from working for Sheila Willcox, she was quite decided that she was going to be an event rider, too; and she has pursued success with single-minded determination ever since. But Mary knows very well that without the loyal and enthusiastic support of her family and close friends, none of her remarkable achievements would have been possible.

Not knowing the first thing about horses, Mary's parents supported her in her decision to set herself up on her own, and bought the premises where she now still runs her yard; this was a considerable financial commitment for them. And when her huge lorry rolls in at any horse trials up or down the country, it could well be Mum at the wheel, and probably with Emily somewhere in tow: although Jill Thomson doesn't in fact much like horses, she has always helped in any other way she possibly can – she even took the HGV test at the age of fifty, so she could drive the new lorry!

Later, impressed by Mary's infectious enthusiasm, her absolute integrity and her modest determination, David King and Gill Robinson joined the team; and it is these qualities in Mary which continue to attract willing sponsors.

Top: Mary stops for a chat with her father: 'William is the only horse in the yard that my father recognises!'

Above: The grin on David's face seems to suggest that babysitting isn't always tedious!

Left: Two working mums! Mary with her mother

Right: On Mary's wedding day 'Wicked Willie' lives up to his stable name

Mum: the lynch-pin

'Mum is a really big part of the team, though she's actually rather scared of horses, and doesn't understand how they think and react. Her support has been invaluable; she's always come to events and helped with the driving. I once went to one on my own, and fell off, and was carted off to hospital, leaving a lorry and two horses behind; since then she's always insisted that someone else who could drive went with me. But my father isn't interested in anything horsey at all, and she never liked to leave him for too long; though now she comes to more competitions – much to his disgust – because she's my main nanny for Emily!

'She often gives the horses their evening feeds at 6pm; the girls finish at 5pm, when Emily and I tend to go home – we live about twenty-five minutes away. She's very practical, and loves doing things like painting, or raking the arena, or pulling up docks – anything, really, except having to touch the horses!

'At competitions she's great, and will keep an eye on the scores, and before I set off across country she'll let me know exactly how I stand. When I've finished she'll generally underplay things – so rather than saying, "Oh, you're bound to win", she'll say "Well, you could well come in fourth, perhaps maybe even better" – and then it's great if you're second or even first!

'She never worries, or fusses over me – we often walk the course together, and far from being anxious about the size of the fences, she'll be working out the best place where she can see as much as possible; when I'm galloping along I'll occasionally see her, out of the corner of my eye, running to her next vantage point! But she never gets wound up, or hassles me; we get on really well, more like sisters.

'She takes complete charge of provisioning the lorry: the food, picnics and drinks. She's also brilliant at cleaning my boots! When we leave an event I drive the wiggly bits because Mum's happier doing the motorway driving, then we'll swop.

'One of her earliest memories of William was when we were at Ferdi's for a dressage lesson, and she was holding him; and William suddenly shot his head up and stood all tall and alert, looking keenly at something in the distance – she says she remembers thinking nervously how big he was, and hoping he wouldn't tread on her feet! – but she couldn't see anything that might have caught his eye. Then eventually she noticed, about five or six fields away, a little dog bouncing through some long grass, and it was this dog which had so riveted his attention!

'Mum's main task now is to have sole charge of Emily when I'm actually competing, or committed to meetings or demonstrations; I can't imagine what we'd do without her – it would be very difficult indeed to keep going!'

My father: background support

'My father came to be a verger in our local church when he was invalided out of the Royal Navy after a serious motorbike accident. He doesn't always treat visitors to the church with the same equanimity, and Mum, who used to help in the tea-shop, was sometimes on the receiving end of their remarks: if they said, "We've just met such a charming man!", she'd reply: "Oh yes! That's my husband!". But if it was "We've just been shown round by this rather strange fellow, who is he?", she'd say, "Oh, that's Mr Thomson…"

'He's so proud when there's a write-up about us in the *Daily Telegraph*, which he reads every day; and so far it's William who has brought me into the limelight the most. With his distinctive white face, he's also the only horse in the yard that Dad ever recognises – though actually Mum isn't very good at knowing which one is which, either! If I'm hacking through the village and I bump into Dad I'll say "OK, Dad, which horse am I on today, then?" – and he won't have a clue, and will just take a pot-shot at any old name, unless I'm on William!'

David: my other half

'David became half-owner of William right at the start, and it's quite amazing that the three horses he's had a share in – Boris, William and Star Appeal – have been my very best. I keep trying to get him involved in more, but he won't have it!

'The fact that William has taken him, and me, to two Olympics, and round the world to big championship events, has brought us so much excitement – and of course he's shared in the disappointments, too. In fact I've known David for as long as I've had William – I quite often call him "William" by mistake! And I tell people that if William had been a human, David wouldn't have had a look-in…!

'David doesn't ride, but likes to lead William round after he's been washed off, say, after a cross-country round; then he feels the proud owner, especially if William went well – which generally he will have! His most striking memory of William is at his second Badminton, at the first veterinary inspection, when he trotted up "…just like a film-star!".

'Obviously it worried him when I continued to compete when I was carrying Emily, but I was regularly checked by my doctor, who was quite easy about it as long as I felt comfortable with it. It's ironic that when I was pregnant I fell off William at Gatcombe, having never done so before; and I came off Conker at Shamley Green jumping the practice fence! Both were completely unexpected, "one-off" accidents. But David knows how determined I am and respects that this is what I want to do; he never hassles or criticises, and has always been completely supportive and encouraging, whatever the circumstances – he has total confidence in William and me!'

Above: Jill Thomson, hoping she won't be left so close to William for too long!
Left: Annie tightening the overgirth; Mary looking anxious, William calm and confident

Sponsor, friend and mainstay

'Gill Robinson came into my life very early on, and has been the very best sponsor and friend that any event rider – that anybody! – could possibly have! She paid for the other half of William, and he quickly became a favourite – though he didn't manage to oust Boris as Gill's number one! Boris was always more cuddly than William. However, William has given us many an excuse for a party! Gill is a very cheerful, sociable sort of person, and is always the first to crack open a bottle of champagne, whether to celebrate or commiserate – and William's career has certainly brought opportunities on both counts!

'I feel my relationship with Gill is probably unique, and certainly very special, and that I'm exceptionally lucky. She never dictates what I should do with the horses, and never criticises; at the most disappointing moments in William's career she's always been cheerful and encouraging: she'll say "Never mind, he'll be fine next time!", never "Oh dear, what did you do wrong?"

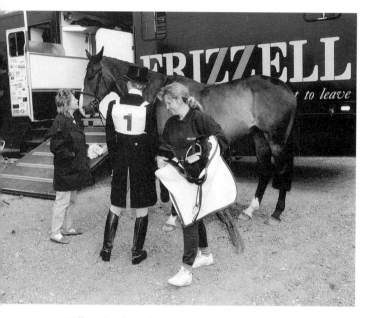

Gill, at her happiest supporting us behind the scenes

'Gill has been all over the world with us, and I feel I know her like a sister. Her commitment and loyalty to me and to the sport of horse trials is really remarkable. She comes to the smallest events, not just the championships, and likes nothing better than to mix at "grass-roots" level with all the grooms and riders; whereas most owners will stay in a hotel or with friends, she and Geoff will live in their motorhome, along with all of us. They experience the highs and the lows at first hand, the worries, say, of having a horse that you think might not make it through the final veterinary inspection so you're up all night with ice-packs – and the relief when it passes! This personal relationship, over so many years and involving several different horses, must be unique.

'Initially Gill sponsored me for four years through the Carphone Group, run by herself and her first husband. Then Gill and I went out on our own for a couple of years while we looked for other sponsorship, and she just helped with the costs of running her own horses. Then we managed to get sponsorship from Frizzell, the international insurance company, so the horses ran under the names of Frizzell Insurance and Gill Robinson; this took the financial pressure off Gill, though she was still very anxious to be a part of it all, and wanted to go at least halves on any new horses that I bought. Now she and Hiscox Insurance sponsor me.

'My abiding memory of her is walking round an event with Geoff, her husband, and their three dogs; she gets as much thrill from watching her younger horses go round the small Novice events as she does from the more experienced ones contest the major championships.'

Gill and Geoff, well-prepared for the often less than clement weather, with two of their ever-present dogs!

Annie's view

'If it hadn't been for William, I'd never have been to so many wonderful places. He's a surprisingly complex character, sometimes very aloof and almost stand-offish, at others obviously needing someone around to help him feel secure. He draws a great deal of confidence from other horses: he can be quite traffic-shy, but is fine if led; and if stabled overnight at an event he'll immediately fall in love with the horse next door, and gets in a terrible panic if it's taken away! He's the sort of horse that likes a consistent routine, and is a gentleman to deal with; he'll spend hours watching the world go by from his barn window, and that's how I always picture him.

'Our first Olympics were a tremendous experience! I was quite anxious about William having to fly out; during team training everyone joked about not wanting their horse to be next to William because they thought he'd get wound up. However, he travelled next to a very experienced Portuguese horse, and we made sure he was hungry beforehand, and he settled down quite happily. The real problem came at Barcelona, because there was no ramp to get the horses off! They rigged up this alarmingly shaky-looking affair, and William came down it at a canter, towing me along behind!

'The routine was much like any other three-day event, though more tiring because of the heat. We all know what happened on the cross-country, and although William's showjumping round has been much criticised, we knew he'd done his best: the fact that he becomes tense is because he's nervous, not because he's ungenuine or careless. So we were very proud of him, because he was still amongst the top ten horses in the world! We stayed in Barcelona for another week, and that was brilliant: I would ride him bareback in my bikini up to the steeplechase course to graze, then back down to the stables for a cool shower together!

Top: Last minute adjustments
before the cross-country at Pratoni
in 1995

Above: Annie and William at home
and (right) in the stables at
Atlanta, surrounded by good luck
letter and cards

'Conditions at the World Championships, on the other hand, were really cramped – in true British spirit we knocked two stables into one for William, leaving me with no tack-room at all! – but William remained, for him, almost laid back. His dressage test was one of the best I've seen him do.

'We know now that his dehydration was an accumulative process, but at the time it was truly alarming to see him in such a state, particularly as normally he made it look so easy. William has always been an incredibly tough, sound horse, and we've never had to worry about whether he would be sound for the final vetting.

'The showjumping was another matter, and when William completely flattened the practice fence all our hearts sank! David Broome helped us rebuild it, and was so calm: he just said, "Come in slowly, Mary, and give him as much room as possible" – and William cleared it well. Lars had suggested that Mary should try riding William into the arena on a long rein so he could have a good look at everything; so he came in gawping around like a giraffe! But he only had two down!

'And then there was Atlanta – as soon as we landed the horses went into quarantine, and this was a new experience for me. Before they were stabled all their clothing was washed, they were examined minutely for parasites, then washed all over with a vinegary solution; their heart and respiration rates and temperature were constantly monitored. The rules were strict: we had only limited access, and then had to wear a paper suit – which terrified William!

'Afterwards we went to Pinetops, where the flies were a real problem; William's boots rubbed, and his girth area became swollen, so we had to use bandages and a sleeve. Otherwise he was very relaxed – and he had an extra feed at night. We never do this at home, but everyone else had one, so he got one, too!

'In the Horse Park the stabling and facilities were brilliant; the organisers had provided everything to make our job easier: washing-down areas, taps everywhere and lungeing rings (which William used for rolling in!).

'In the dressage he gave the performance of a lifetime – I was in tears, it was so fabulous. Later I walked the cross-country, and I thought it was well within William's ability, but didn't like the slippery terrain. I was up at 4.30am on cross-country day to feed William. Mary didn't want him plaited, and she always bandages him, so there wasn't much else to do. We know each other so well now, and just get on with our jobs and wait quietly for countdown. Mary set off at 7.30am, and almost immediately I had a panic because no shuttle turned up to take me to the steeplechase; eventually I set off on foot, though luckily someone gave me a lift. William looked good; the extra stops on phase C had certainly refreshed him.

'I watched his round from a monitor: when he stopped I felt completely numb. Then I just wanted them both back in one piece. When they came in William had pulled both his front shoes loose, so I was kept busy with Icetight and ice poultices on his feet, just to be on the safe side; and the next day he was blooming! He really is the toughest horse imaginable!

'What can we say about the showjumping? After the Hague and Pratoni we'd thought he was learning to cope – but sadly this wasn't so. In spite of this, Atlanta was a fantastic experience. Atlanta had much more buzz than Barcelona – and what really made it for me was the opening ceremony, marching into the stadium with all the other athletes: American razzamatazz is really quite something!'

Sponsors, past and present
Mary is the first to acknowledge how much she owes to Gill Robinson, whose very generous sponsorship has continued throughout her entire career. Mary's most recent sponsors are Hiscox, world leaders in bloodstock insurance, and experts in a number of other areas notably specialist professional products, fine art, character properties and their contents. They are the insurers of many stately homes – several of which are the venues for horse trials.

David also has a half share in her two top horses, William and Star Appeal, as he did in Boris; his commitment and support have been 100 per cent throughout. Because of this Mary has never been under quite the same pressure as many event riders who have to run large strings of horses for many different owners, and buy and sell horses in order to make a living. She is most grateful to Hiscox Insurance, who '…came in at the beginning of 1998 and took on four horses: King Solomon, King Patrick and King Richard; and William as a good, reliable campaigner who by association as well as – hopefully! – consistent results would put their name to the fore. They have been brilliant, because during the first few months of their going public, three of the horses fell by the wayside: Solomon went lame and will be off for some time, Richard was kicked in the knee, and I sold Patrick! They knew that was my intention, but even so, it's only good old William who's loyally trucking on!'

Mary's trainers
'For the dressage I've always got on extremely well with Ferdi Eilberg, who has been enormously helpful. I remember having lessons with Conker [King Kong] who on more than one occasion was so wound up that all I could do was canter a twenty-metre circle for an hour! But Ferdi could always help me get the very best out of my horses.

'For showjumping William and I have been to different people because it's a difficult phase for him, and it's my weakest one, too. I think a rider benefits enormously by going to

'I have known William for quite a few years, and worked with him during his eventing career.

He is such an enthusiastic horse when it comes to working. I will never forget his expression after his cross-country round in Barcelona 1992. He looked like he wanted to go round again! Sometimes at big events we had a bit of a problem controlling his energies and making him show off his excellent walk.

'His will to work, and good health, have made him a great horse for so many years, and "he ain't finished yet!" '

Ferdi Eilberg

HORSE OF THE YEAR SHOW 400,000 READERS EVERY WEEK
full reports and pictures from Wembley

I FREELY ADMIT THAT THE BEST OF MY FUN I OWE IT TO HORSE AND HOUND – Whyte-Melville

HORSE and HOUND

October 5 1995
EVERY THURSDAY £1.30

EURO GOLD
Glory for Britain's team

LAMMTARRA
the brave heart's Arc

PLUS:
- Houghton Sales
- Autumn hunting
- Osberton Horse Trials
- VET– leg injuries to show jumpers

Britain's only equestrian new

HORSE & HOUN

Every

Horse Trials answers critics after triple fatality

HORSE and HOUND

MAY 14 1992 EVERY THURSDAY £1.15

I FREELY ADMIT THAT THE BEST OF MY FUN I OWE IT TO HORSE AND HOUND – Whyte-Melville

WILLIAM YOU'RE A KING!

Mary Thomson's Badminton triumph:
rts, results,
es galore

---

tcombe

Eventing
SUPPLEMENT
WITH EVENTING APRIL 1997

LEARN TO EVENT WITH MARY KING

All you need to
before you tac
your first BHTA
horse trials

Britain's Dublin show jumping

The 1997 Mitsubishi Motors Badminton Horse Trials

MITSUBISHI MOTORS

May 8th - 11th
Programme £3

Save the Children

THE BADMINTON HORSE TRIALS
FOR THE MITSUBISHI MOTORS TROPHY 1993

PROGRAMME £2.50

MAY 6th - 9th

HORSE and HO

I FREELY ADMIT THAT THE BEST OF MY FUN I OWE IT TO HORSE

AUGUST 15 1991 EVERY THURSDAY £1.10

Mary holds Gatcombe title

Renowned throughout the horse trials world as an indomitable partnership, William and Mary have been front cover subjects for ten years; Ian Stark recognised their talent early on: '… at Badminton as an eight-year-old he showed such promise and star quality I knew we were seeing the beginning of an illustrious career'

different trainers – you take in little bits of what is most relevant to you and your horse, and learn from the amalgam. Lars Sederholm has been by far the most helpful. He is the most amazing person, and can really look into a horse's mind; his method is geared towards building up the horse's own confidence and getting it to believe in its own capability, rather than pressurising it to jump bigger and better. This suits William very well, since his problem is in his brain rather than his actual ability.

'Over the years I've had a lot of help from different quarters: Kenneth Clawson was very helpful early in William's career; I learned a great deal from Steve Hadley, who became the official trainer for the event team; and from Captain Mark Phillips. Even to this day, if the Captain is at a competition he'll always help at a practice fence, and is so obliging – he'll say odd little things regarding what he sees in your riding or your horse's way of going, which can sometimes make all the difference to your performance on the day.'

William in the public eye

A horse of William's eye-catching presence and magnetic personality is inevitably much sought after for advertising purposes by producers of horse products, clothing and feedstuffs. In particular the many firms who sponsor the British team at a championship event want the riders and horses to pose with their goods in order to promote them. Team training always provides a good opportunity for photocalls, and William is generally in most demand:

William's distinctive white face and characteristic pose gazing into the distance with his ears pricked make him a firm favourite with the photographers. Mary has been on call many times to model team uniform – some more flattering than others!

'He's such an attractive horse, and so good at posing, always keeping exceptionally still, and brilliant at putting his ears forwards, and gazing into the distance – the photographers just love him! One of the horses in the Mitsubishi trophy is modelled on William; though I don't think it's too good a likeness: in the figure the horse is certainly gazing "up and beyond", but is rather short on the leg and just isn't tall enough altogether.

'Many artists have wanted to paint him, and there have been some really good likenesses made of him – and some not so good! Amongst the best must be that by Bridget Anne Smart, depicting the heads of my two favourite top horses, William and Boris.

'Sometimes William is used as part of a first prize in, say, magazine promotion competitions: *Horse and Pony* ran a quiz where the winner was given a "lunge lesson with Mary King": William is nearly always the most popular of my horses and has a huge fan club, and it's a great thrill for a young person to have the opportunity to sit on William on the lunge! And he's very good in that respect, and stays quiet and calm; I think he understands that he must only trot and canter steadily on a circle – and usually they're quite reasonable riders. I think he'd get anxious and jumpy if you put up a very novice rider who tended to cling on a bit. I can't plonk Emily on his back and lead her round the yard, like I can with the other horses, because she's something different and you can see that this fills him with alarm. If someone were anxious or nervous he would sense this immediately and probably try to rush off; but as long as the rider is reasonably knowledgeable and competent, he'd be fine!'

Left: Still smiling: the showjumping isn't always unreliable!

Right: To spend some time in close contact with William is a huge thrill for any young fan! Kate Sutton won first prize in a competition run by Horse and Pony *magazine to spend a day at Mary's yard*

'It is not often that any sport is lucky enough to benefit from a "household name". In horse trials William has become one of those names. A model of consistency in the dressage, William is better known for his long economic stride devouring fence after fence across the country. Were it not for his infamous tendencies in the showjumping on the final day of the three-day event he would have been one of the sport's "all time greats".

'The length of his career speaks volumes for how easy he has found his task and for Mary's care and attention to detail in every aspect of his well-being and training.'

Captain Mark Phillips

'When William arrived in Devon, he had a wonderful presence about him, even as a five-year-old. As he came down the ramp on that very first day my immediate reaction was that he was a beautiful horse, but why did he have to be so big? Yet another big horse for me to struggle with! Even as a baby he was a gentle giant, really enjoying the new challenges Mary gave him.

'Together we've travelled thousands of miles, to Italy, France, Spain, Ireland, Holland and the United States. We've experienced all kinds of transport, from my sister Julie's little lorry to flying in jumbo jets. We've stayed in 5-star accommodation, and in places that didn't even deserve half a star! William got quite used to me turning up at all hours of the day and night, sometimes straight from a party in my dress and wellies!

'William, Mary and I did fourteen three-day events over the years I worked with them, including two European Championships, one World Championship and two Olympic Games. Quite an achievement!

'William will always hold a special place in my heart. I still see him and support him at as many competitions as I can. I visited many places round the world with him for the first time. I have made lots of friends along the way, many of whom I will keep for the rest of my life. None of this would have been possible without Mary and Gill's support, and I will always be grateful to them for the experiences I had while I was William's groom.'

Annie Collings

HOME LIFE

Mary's yard at Thorn Farm, on the edge of the tiny village of Salcombe Regis, is like a green oasis in the midst of the glorious Devonshire countryside. Hanging baskets fill the evening air with their scent and add a lively touch of colour, and contented faces poke out of every stable door to scrutinise with inquisitive interest any visitor who might come strolling in. The stable cat lounges sleepily in the summer sunshine. You can almost feel the sea – the coast is only half a mile away – and the surrounding lanes, full of wildflowers, and rolling green hills are ideal for fittening work. The local farmers do their bit to help Mary, too, in terms of leasing her additional grazing and providing suitable gallops for the horses' fastwork.

All in all it's a wonderful place, where horses young and old – both the inexperienced five-year-old and the seasoned campaigner – have the peace and ambience to develop and flourish to their full capability under the care of Mary and her team. But life at the yard wasn't always quite as it is today…

The peaceful rural surroundings and undulating grassland provide the ideal training ground for both young and experienced horses alike; the proximity of the sea is a bonus!

From pigs and pony rides to Olympic fame

Mary's decision to set up her own business and become an event rider seemed an impossibility to her parents: they lived in a small cottage owned by the church, with no land or stables, and they had very little money for that sort of enterprise. Undeterred, Mary set about looking for a suitable premises, and eventually found a disused yard about half a mile from her parents' house. Originally it had been a part of Thorn Farm, and they discovered that the farmer who owned the buildings was happy to rent out the odd cowshed for a very small amount. The whole site comprises three acres in all, and the buildings had once been part of a working farm; in fact there were still pigs in one of the barns!

'You could see where the old stalls for the farm horses had been, and they obviously used to milk cows because one of our first jobs was to get rid of the concrete troughs and metal cow-chains – Mum and I spent hours wielding a pneumatic drill! Clearing them out took ages because they were just full of old scrap and rubbish – I should think they'd lain empty for a very long time – and the yard itself was completely overgrown with brambles and nettles.

'We made a couple of stables, and bit by bit converted more of the sheds, and I built up quite a little business, taking in liveries, teaching, and buying and selling horses. Eventually the farmer moved the pigs out, which was a huge improvement – their muck used to run down the middle of the yard, and I'm sure this encouraged the rats, which would scamper about my feet when I went to feed the horses in the evening – horrible! The only good thing was that my young horses were never afraid of pigs again!

'Then out of the blue the farmer decided to sell "my" yard and buildings, which was quite a shock! Whether to buy was a big decision for us; but our solicitor advised us that we had sitting tenant's rights, since we'd run our business there for the requisite number of years, so we went ahead. This is where my parents were such a help, putting up the capital to purchase the buildings. This was a big step for me: my own yard and business – and a far cry from the verger's daughter begging rides on other people's ponies!

'The countryside round here is great for fittening work, and in fact the hardest thing was to find an area flat enough for the dressage and jump schooling, so it was a great relief when eventually I was able to put down a proper surface. Besides, in recent years the spring months have been so wet it's been impossible to ride over fields, however well disposed the farmer – quite apart from the risk of straining precious legs in deep going.

'The local farmers are enormously supportive. My three acres are adequate for turning the horses out during the competition season, but for their longer holidays I rent land from Mark Preston and Bob Elliott. I also rely on friendly farmers for the horses' fastwork: the

Coles family in Harcombe and the Bakers in Sidmouth both have large sloping fields that I use for galloping – in sight and smell of the sea, too, which is lovely! If the ground gets really hard in the summer then we load the horses up and go over to Musbury, near Axminster, to the all-weather gallop belonging to Simon Dutfield, the racehorse trainer.

'I really love living down here; it's great being in an area where there aren't any other eventing yards! This may seem strange, but when you go up to the Midlands there are so many horsey yards that you never seem to get away from the same old talk; and when you go out in the evening everybody is still discussing everybody else's horses, and inevitably there's a lot of backbiting. Down here you miss out on the gossip, which is a bit disappointing sometimes, and in the winter we get a bit behind with what is going on! – but I would always much prefer this comparative peace to living further up-country.

'It does also mean that we have to get up an hour or two earlier on competition days to travel the extra distance, but once you're all in the lorry and on the way it doesn't seem to matter much whether you're going for two hours or five. This is where Mum comes into her own; she does love driving, and never seems to get tired, so we take it in turns to drive and to entertain Emily, if she's awake.

'We're looking for a property closer to the yard, now; it would be lovely to live "on site", especially with a second child on the way, because it does get a bit tedious driving back and forth from home to Sidmouth; though I'm so used to it that really you just get on and do it. And in many ways it's quite relaxing coming back home and having a complete break from the yard. We shut up the yard at 6pm, and start again at 7 in the morning; Annie used to live just a mile down the road, and Becky, who's taken over from her, is just as close, so if there is a problem – if one of the horses looks colicky, or ill – there's someone near to hand.'

William's day 'William has just been turned out on his holidays, and at the moment is being very awkward about being caught; the pink bits on his nose burn very easily if there's any sun, and blister badly, so I put on some sun-block cream, and fly-spray when the flies are bad. All the others come up quite happily to have this done, and I think just to be friendly – but not William. So you go trailing around after him; he lets you get up to him eventually, but for the first couple of weeks of his holiday he's always difficult: he'll get friendly again, soon! Normally he likes being fiddled about with – groomed and plaited and trimmed – but he knows this is holiday, so just wants to be left alone.

'Of all the horses here he loves Lillie best, and I'm sure he thinks he's the father of her foal!

Home life for William
Top: Enjoying his daily turnout – with a companion nearby so that he doesn't worry

'The day starts for the horses when Becky arrives at about 7.15am, when she feeds them all. William just loves his food, and as soon as he hears the car he'll look out over the door, watching eagerly and whinnying; he gets quite agitated while he's waiting for it, and will succumb to his naughty habit of weaving – once he has it, he's fine!

'He has Spillers horse cubes and a coarse mix with a bit of chaff, and he's rather pushy when you take it into the stable – he knows really that he has to wait until it's tipped into his manger, but he'll always see if he can get away with grabbing a quick mouthful from the bucket first! When you tip it in, he will go for it with his mouth open and grab a huge mouthful, so big that half of it all spills out again! He never leaves any, and he'll also spend hours sifting through his bedding for any that might have fallen over the rim; his manger is a shallow trough which runs along the back wall, and he'll make such a thorough job of working through his bed that he sweeps a shallow channel along the floor, the length of the trough!

'He's then mucked out while he has his morning haynet of dampened hay. When he was younger he'd be all keen and ready to go out on exercise when he'd finished eating; however, this has definitely changed over the years, and now he's older he likes to have a snooze after his breakfast, and will either lie down, or prop his bum firmly against the far corner and have a nap standing up – and he'll get quite grumpy if you try and tack him up before he's ready! So now he goes out later in the morning with the second lot, after his sleep!

'But he's still so enthusiastic in his work; whether schooling, or jumping, or galloping, he's always very purposeful and happy to be working. He switches off a bit if he's at the back when we hack out, and if I'm riding him and leading another he'll pull frightful faces if it bumps him; but generally he's most amenable, and slots into the pecking order without fuss. He's very much a gentleman and well mannered in that respect.

'He's pretty much on his toes even now, and always takes notice of things, but when he was younger he was extremely sharp and alert, and anything strange would make him a bit anxious – even now a group of visitors round the yard will worry him, and make him weave a bit. Back then it was difficult to keep the weight on him; he would always eat up, but I suppose because he was so often on edge he was quite lean. He used to be really quite frightened of cattle and sheep, or an odd-looking dog, or people he thought looked unusual; he would snort and quiver all over, and you'd feel his heart thumping – he just couldn't help himself. This fearful reaction to outside things was why he was so easily distracted in the showjumping, and by crowds of people. So although he may seem calm, and almost aloof, he's a funny mixture because inside he's worrying about so many things.

'He's always been ticklish, and as a result is tense when his saddle is put on, putting his ears back and wiggling his head, but it doesn't mean anything. As a rule I ride three or four horses in a day, and William now goes out the second or third; the girls tack him up and get him ready, and they do the hacking out. He's very helpful in the stable; we always pick out the horses' feet before they're brought out into the yard, and when you go in with a hoof-pick William will lift each foot up in turn for you.

'Now that he's older I still school him to make sure he's working with proper engagement and suppleness, but I certainly ride him less. As a youngster he was so exuberant, always in a hurry, and had this enormous power from his quarters which would actually propel him forwards too much and onto his forehand; I used to have to work him for hours on the flat to teach him to be calmer and to carry himself, and not to run along on his forehand and be so strong in my hand. Gradually he learned to use his power to carry his own weight, and then he was so much easier to ride; but he was eight before I got the feeling that he was learning true engagement and true self-carriage, and it took all that time for the schooling and flatwork to come through in competitions.

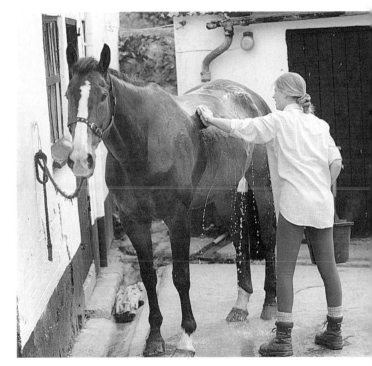

'He has stayed remarkably sound and supple for a more mature horse, but isn't as exuberant now, and I have to work quite hard at home to make sure he's really "coming through" in order to keep his paces impressive so as to get the good marks in competition – obviously I insist that he gives his best every time I school him, because if you want to be successful you have got to be thorough. He's lovely to work because he's always willing to please

William is quite happy to be washed, trimmed and plaited, and (overleaf) he enjoys nothing more than Mary giving him a jolly good brush – and particularly a scratch on the face!

and knows the movements inside out, but whereas when he was younger he offered lots of sparkle and exuberance, now I have to work a bit harder to achieve it.

'What does he like doing best? Galloping and jumping over big fences! He finds galloping easy, and he has such a powerful physique, you feel he just relishes using his strength and fitness to attack a big course – he eats up the fences like a tiger, looking for the next one as he jumps, ears pricked, bounding along. The only other horse that has ever given me a similar feeling is Star Appeal.

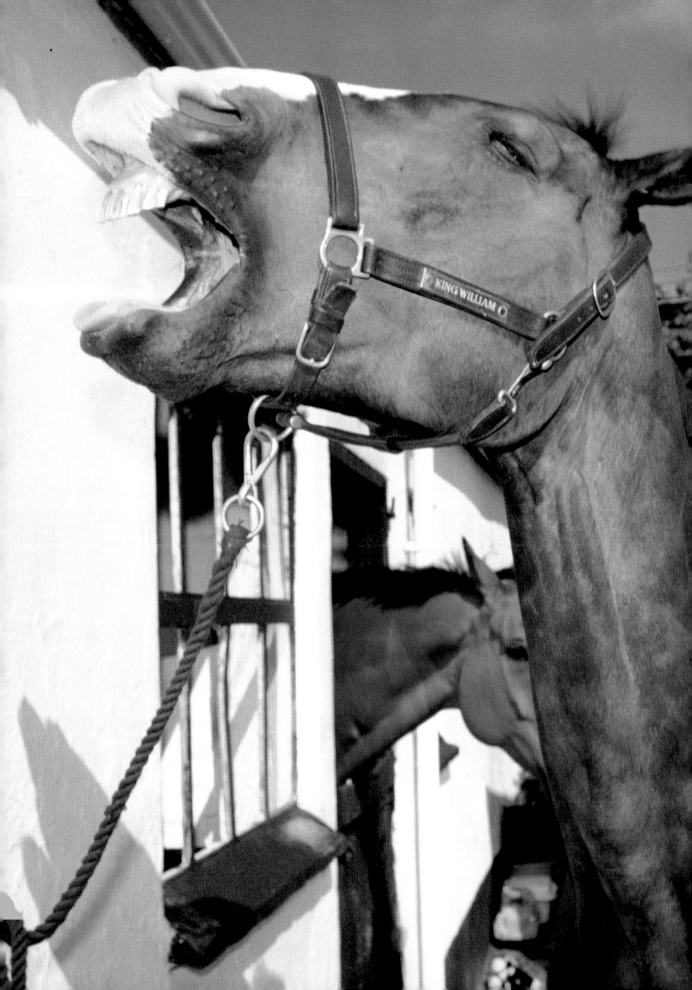

'When we get back from exercise William will just stand while you go and get his headcollar; we have an old bath in the yard which is always full of fresh water, and as soon as you take his bridle off he will go over and plunge his head into it and drink – he doesn't like his headcollar on until he's finished, which I dare say isn't very professional, but he hasn't taken off yet!

'Then he's washed down if necessary, and goes out in the paddock for an hour – and he needs a companion, otherwise he'll whinny and run up and down the fence and get quite agitated; it need only be someone in an adjoining field, but on his own he'll worry – and this just shows how insecure he is at heart which, given how bold and brave he is across country, is surprising. He's good to catch, as long as you leave him for his full hour: if you try and get him after just twenty minutes, he will wander off and look grumpy!

'After this he comes in and is groomed – and then it is lunch-time, and he'll shout and stamp around and weave a bit if he thinks you might be late or have forgotten! He just has Spillers cubes at that time. The afternoon is siesta time, when the girls catch up with odd jobs around the yard.

'Our farrier at the moment is Clive Evans, and because William has quite shallow heels in front Clive will shoe him with wide-web shoes, and leave the heels as long as possible; he will have two stud holes in each shoe, but will only wear studs for competitions. William is fine with Clive, but is otherwise quite nervous of men; he's definitely scared of the vet, and even gets quite anxious with any male work-experience pupils we might have – I remember one taking the tack into William's stable to get him ready for me, and he was gone for ages, until eventually I went over to see what was up; the student hadn't tied him up, and William was obviously scared of this strange fellow, and kept walking off round the stable every time the poor chap approached him – not kicking or turning his backside, but just wouldn't let him touch him!

'At 5pm he is skipped out, and the girls go; then he has his night haynet, a couple of buckets of water, and Mum or I will give him and the others their evening feeds.

'His stable has a window at the back, and a third, small one which looks out over the campsite; this one is quite high, but William will stand up as tall as he can so as to be able to look out of it, and he obviously likes to do this because you will often see him there, gazing out.

'So he's a real gentleman to "do" at home, and no trouble to manage. And he is a groom's delight to produce: with his powerful, muscular body and glorious dapples, I don't think he has ever not looked a picture!'

William's competition days

'William probably knows when it's his turn for a competition because we generally plait the horses the evening before, but I don't think this upsets him unduly because I've never known him leave his breakfast! He's always enthusiastic and excited about going anywhere, and as soon as he's all dressed up he'll bound up the ramp – I think if you just opened the stable door he'd actually go out of the gate, into the road and up the lorry ramp all on his own!

'He travels very well, on the whole; just occasionally he'll have moments when he seems more tense, and will weave a little bit – he'll be quite calm, then all at once he'll get twitchy and nervous, perhaps in anticipation.

'As he's got older he's become easier to handle; when he was a youngster he was always so exuberant and full of energy, and would come bursting out of the lorry and down the ramp, and in order to have any chance of performing a reasonable dressage test I would lunge him for some time so he could burn off any surplus energy, and to encourage him to take a deep breath and relax a bit! Then he'd go back in the lorry for a while, and hopefully by the time I got on him he'd be even more relaxed and not too strong in my hand.

Cattle used to scare the living daylights out of William, and as a youngster, a skittish heifer would have sent him down the field at full gallop!

'Lungeing him seems to be less necessary now he's older, though I do lunge him a bit to loosen up his muscles. However, he knows the different phases now, so he's not worried at all when I get ready for the dressage; but when we put the cross-country bandages on, he starts to quiver in excitement. Once I'm in the saddle, he's fine. Generally he settles down afterwards quite happily, though I do remember that in Pratoni he'd obviously got really wound up and couldn't cope – I suppose because we'd won gold the crowd was cheering particularly loudly, and there were endless photos. He was weaving and pacing about and rolling, and really going quite dotty, which was a worry for everybody! In the end the team vet gave him a sedative, which was just what he needed because from then on he was fine, even when it had obviously worn off – he just needed that "space" and help to calm down.'

'William is always enthusiastic in his work, and always happy to do whatever you ask of him – even a photocall!', says Mary

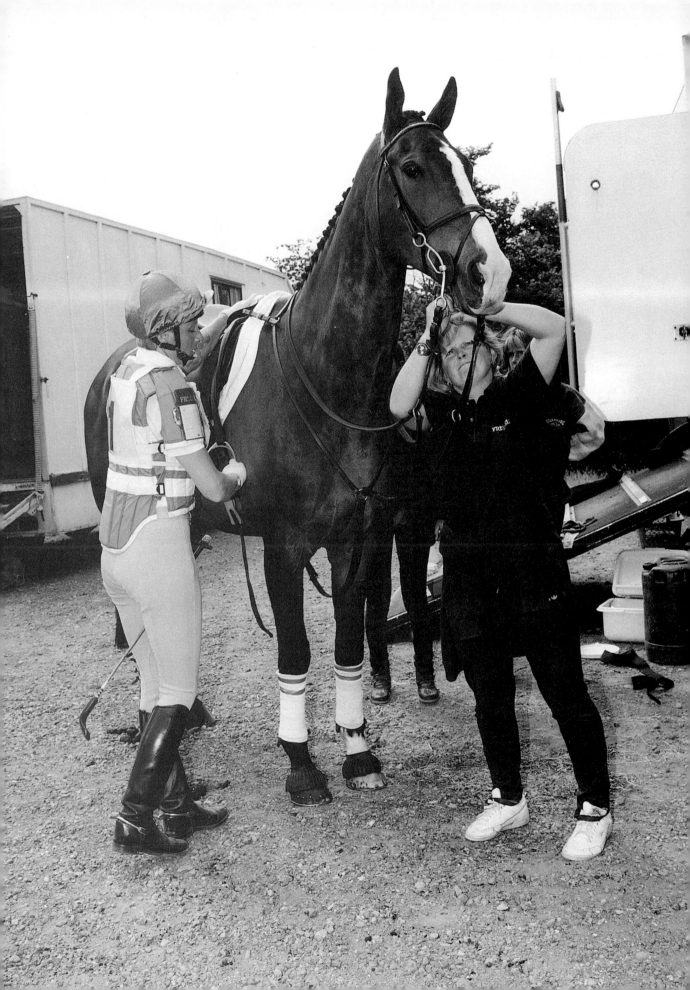

BHTA RESULTS

A listing of all competitions in which King William gained a top placing

KEY

Classes:

NO	Novice
IN	Intermediate
AD	Advanced
BC (N)	British Championship (Novice)
OI	Open Intermediate
CA	Championship Advanced
IRF	Intermediate Regional Final
SOC	Scottish Open Championship

CCI   Concours Complet International
(followed by star rating)

CCIO   Concours Complet International Open

NOTES

Where a number follows the class abbreviation this shows that the competition was divided into sections and indicates in which section King William competed.

King William gained points, although he was not in the top placings, when he competed at Badminton in 1993 and at Atlanta in 1996; these are listed as 'allocated'.

EVENT	DATE	CLASS	PLACE	POINTS	EVENT	DATE	CLASS	PLACE	POINTS
LULWORTH CASTLE	01Oct88	NO2	1	6	BADMINTON	05May94	CCI****	11	50
BARNSLEY PARK	18Mar89	N04	2	5	MILTON KEYNES	25Jun94	A01	2	22
PORTMAN	30Mar89	N02	3	4	ALTHORP PARK	02Jul94	A01	6	14
STON EASTON	01Apr89	N02	3	4	THE HAGUE	27Jul94	CCIO	4	160
ERMINGTON	05Apr89	N01	1	6	LULWORTH CASTLE	24Sep94	0102	1	12
RAGLEY HALL	20May89	IN01	1	12	WESTON PARK	07Oct94	A01	1	24
DODINGTON	16Jul89	IN04	1	12	PEPER HAROW	11Mar95	0102	1	12
LE LION D'ANGERS	22Oct89	CCI**	5	22	BELTON PARK	08Apr95	A05	1	24
PORTMAN	29Mar90	0101	1	12	BRIGSTOCK	15Apr95	A03	1	24
BRAMHAM	07Jun90	CCI***	6	35	BADMINTON	04May95	CCI****	14	50
DODINGTON	15Jul90	0I02	6	2	THIRLESTANE CASTLE	19Aug95	S0C01	1	24
SHAMLEY GREEN	21Jul90	0I01	4	6	SOMERLEYTON	09Sep95	0101	1	12
LOCKO PARK	04Aug90	BC(I)01	2	13	PRATONI	28Sep95	CCIO	3	170
TETBURY	15Sep90	A02	2	22	ALDON	15Mar96	0101	3	8
BLENHEIM	27Sep90	CCI***	9	25	DYNES HALL	31Mar96	A01	1	24
DYNES HALL	24Mar91	A02	3	20	BELTON PARK	13Apr96	A04	2	22
DODINGTON	14Jul91	0I01	5	4	ATLANTA *(allocated)*	26Jul96			50
AUCHINLECK	31Jul91	A02	2	22	ATLANTA	26Jul96	CCIO	12	25
GATCOMBE PARK	09Aug91	CA01	1	30	GATCOMBE PARK	30Aug96	CA01	1	30
ALDON	21Mar92	0I02	1	6	LULWORTH CASTLE	28Sep96	A01	5	16
KINGS SOMBORNE	05Apr92	A03	4	18	PEPER HAROW	08Mar97	0I02	1	12
BRIGSTOCK	17 Apr92	A03	3	20	ALDON	14Mar97	0I02	1	12
BADMINTON	07May92	CCI****	1	90	GATCOMBE	22Mar97	A101	2	10
BARCELONA	25Jul92	CCIO	9	6	DAUNTSEY	05Apr97	A01	4	18
ALDON	20Mar93	0102	1	12	BELTON PARK	12Apr97	A02	4	18
BELTON PARK	17Apr93	A02	3	20	BICTON	25Apr97	A02	1	24
BADMINTON *(allocated)*	06May93			25	PUNCHESTOWN	19May97	CCI***	6	50
BRIGHTLING PARK	10Jul93	A01	2	22	CHANTILLY	22Jun97	CIC**	1	55
ALTHORP PARK	17Jul93	A01	1	24	CORNBURY PARK	26Jul97	A04	5	16
STOWE	24Jul93	0102	1	12	GATCOMBE PARK	01Aug97	CIC***	8	13
GATCOMBE PARK	13Aug93	CA01	8	13	THIRLESTANE CASTLE	16Aug97	S0C01	8	10
THIRLESTANE CASTLE	21Aug93	SOC01	9	8	BLENHEIM	04Sep97	CCI***	3	80
TAUNTON	18Sep93	0101	2	10	TWESELDOWN (1)	13Mar98	0101	3	8
LULWORTH CASTLE	25 Sep93	0101	1	12	ALDON	20Mar98	0101	1	12
WESTON PARK	08Oct93	A01	3	20	GATCOMBE	28Mar98	A101	2	10
BISHOP BURTON	16Oct93	A01	3	20	BELTON PARK	17Apr98	A01	1	24
PEPER HAROW	12Mar94	0101	1	12	BICTON	01May98	A02	2	22
ALDON	18Mar94	0101	1	12	SAVERNAKE	16May98	A02	2	22
STON EASTON	26Mar94	A03	2	22	LONGLEAT	29May98	0102	2	10
BELTON PARK	16Apr94	A01	7	12					

William is so experienced now, as soon as the Porter boots go on he knows that it is cross-country day and will quiver in anticipation

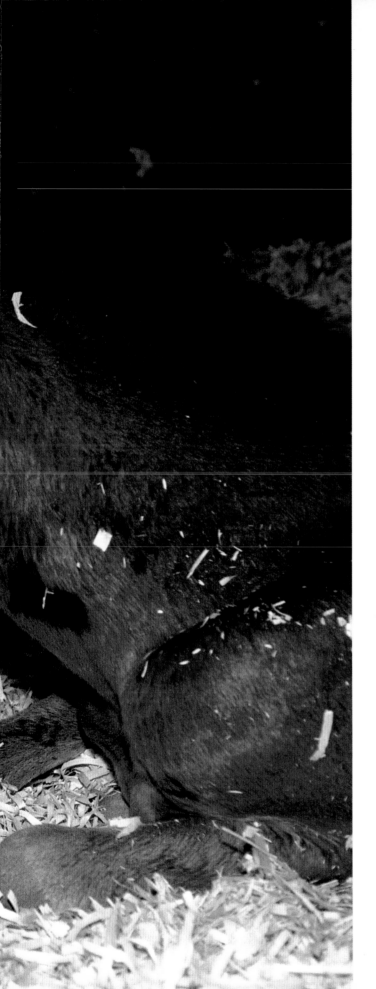

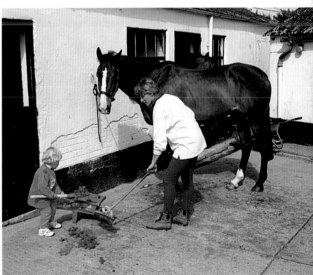

Left: Emily has made it her job to check Lillie's foal, Nancy, every day; she has 'backed' her, too – while Nancy was lying down! – though Nancy is maybe wise to this now, and sometimes keeps her distance

Top: Small, medium and large: Emily, Nancy and Lillie

Above: Starting young! Mary's daughter learns about life in a top eventing yard

A round-up of all William's results, Intermediate and above

EVENT	DATE	CLASS	PLACE	POINTS	EVENT	DATE	CLASS	PLACE	POINTS
BICTON	29Apr89	IN03		52.00	LULWORTH CASTLE	25Sep93	0101	1	33.00
RAGLEY HALL	20May89	IN01	1	41.00	WESTON PARK	08Oct93	A01	3	60.00
DODINGTON	16Jul89	IN04	1	41.00	BISHOP BURTON	16Oct93	A01	3	62.00
FROME	22Jul89	IN03		29.00	PEPER HAROW	12Mar94	0101	1	48.00
LOCKO PARK	05Aug89	BC(N)01	NR	0.00	ALDON	18Mar94	0101	1	36.00
PEPER HAROW	03Mar90	0I0I		55.00	STON EASTON	26Mar94	A03	2	63.00
CROOKHAM	09Mar90	0102		99.00	DYNES HALL	03Apr94	A02		45.00
PORTMAN	29Mar90	0101	1	26.00	BELTON PARK	16Apr94	A01	7	58.00
STON EASTON	31Mar90	0I01		34.00	BADMINTON	05May94	CCI****01	11	75.00
BELTON PARK	07Apr90	A05		142.00	MILTON KEYNES	25Jun94	A01	2	55.00
KINGS SOMBORNE	21Apr90	A02		32.00	ALTHORP PARK	02Jul94	A01	6	50.00
BICTON	28Apr90	A02		45.00	THE HAGUE	27Jul94	CCI001	4	64.80
RAGLEY HALL	06May90	IRF01		0.00	LULWORTH CASTLE	24Sep94	0102	1	29.00
TIDWORTH	24May90	0102		58.00	WESTON PARK	07Oct94	A01	1	41.00
BRAMHAM	07Jun90	CCI**01	6	80.00	PEPER HAROW	11Mar95	0102	1	36.00
DODINGTON	15Jul90	0102	6	38.00	ALDON	17Mar95	0101	NR	0.00
SHAMLEY GREEN	21Jul90	0101	4	40.00	BELTON PARK	08Apr95	A05	1	34.00
LOCKO PARK	04Aug90	BC(I)01	2	46.00	BRIGSTOCK	15Apr95	A03	1	39.00
GATCOMBE PARK	12Aug90	A01		31.00	BADMINTON	04May95	CCI****01	14	76.05
THIRLESTANE CASTLE	18Aug90	A01	10	54.00	DYNES HALL	16Jul95	A01		54.00
ICKWORTH	01Sep90	A02		39.00	SHAMLEY GREEN	21Jul95	A02		25.00
TETBURY	15Sep90	A02	2	43.00	DAUNTSEY	28Jul95	A01		26.00
BLENHEIM	27Sep90	CCI**01	9	72.00	GATCOMBE PARK	04Aug95	CA01		32.00
CROOKHAM	08Mar91	0101		32.00	THIRLESTANE CASTLE	19Aug95	SOC01	1	41.00
ALDON	16Mar91	0102		33.00	SOMERLEYTON	09Sep95	0101	1	30.00
DYNES HALL	24Mar91	A02	3	58.00	PRATONI	28Sep95	CCI001	3	47.25
BELTON PARK	06Apr91	A03		65.00	PEPER HAROW	09Mar96	A101		28.00
SOUTH OF ENGLAND	20Apr91	A01	9	77.00	ALDON	15Mar96	0101	3	42.00
BADMINTON	02May91	CCI****01	37	156.95	GATCOMBE	23Mar96	AI01		35.00
MONTACUTE	06Jul91	0101		32.00	DYNES HALL	31Mar96	A01	1	44.00
DODINGTON	14Jul91	0101	5	36.00	BELTON PARK	13Apr96	A04	2	46.00
EGLINTON	27Jul91	A01		25.00	BADMINTON	02May96	CCI****01		55.60
AUCKINLECK	31Jul91	A02	2	49.00	ATLANTA	26Jul96	CCI****01	12	118.00
GATCOMBE PARK	09Aug91	CA01	1	46.00	LULWORTH CASTLE	28Sep96	A01	5	43.00
ALDON	21Mar92	0102	4	47.00	PEPER HAROW	08Mar97	0102	1	33.00
KINGS SOMBORNE	05Apr92	A03	4	56.00	ALDON	14Mar97	0102	1	36.00
BELTON PARK	11Apr92	A02		27.00	GATCOMBE	22Mar97	A101	2	37.00
BRIGSTOCK	17Apr92	A03	3	41.00	DAUNTSEY	05Apr97	A01	4	56.00
BADMINTON	07May92	CCI****01	1	60.80	BELTON PARK	12Apr97	A02	4	41.00
DODINGTON	29Jun92	AI02		34.00	BICTON	25Apr97	A02	1	42.00
SAVERNAKE	04Jul92	A01	19	60.00	PUNCHESTOWN	19May97	CCI***01	6	56.20
ALDON	20Mar93	0102	1	40.00	CHANTILLY	22Jun97	CIC**01	1	51.40
BELTON PARK	17Apr93	A02	3	47.00	CORNBURY PARK	26Jul97	A04	5	37.00
CORNBURY PARK	24Apr93	A02		43.00	THIRLESTANE CASTLE	16Aug97	SOC01	8	45.00
BADMINTON	06May93	CCI****01	20	76.00	BLENHEIM	04Sep97	CCI***01	3	60.20
BRIGHTLING PARK	10Jul93	A01	2	46.00	TWESELDOWN (1)	13Mar98	0101	3	31.00
STOWE	24Jul93	0102	1	28.00	ALDON	20Mar98	0101	1	28.00
DAUNTSEY	30Jul93	A03		31.00	GATCOMBE	28Mar98	AI01	2	33.00
GATCOMBE PARK	13Aug93	C401	8	56.00	DYNES HALL	05Apr98	A01		76.00
ALTHORP PARK	17Aug93	A01	1	34.00	BELTON PARK	17Apr98	A01	1	40.00
THIRLESTANE CASTLE	21Aug93	SOC01	9	48.00	BICTON	01May98	A02	2	40.00
BURGHLEY	02Sep93	CCI****01		43.00	SAVERNAKE	16May98	A02	2	39.00
TAUNTON	18Sep93	0101	2	33.00	PENTON	23May98	0I02		18.00

'King William is one of those horses that "looks the part". His record speaks for itself, and I will always remember his elegance in the dressage and his fantastic stride and cross-country performances. A horse is only as good as its rider – William and Mary made a memorable partnership.'

Ginny Elliot

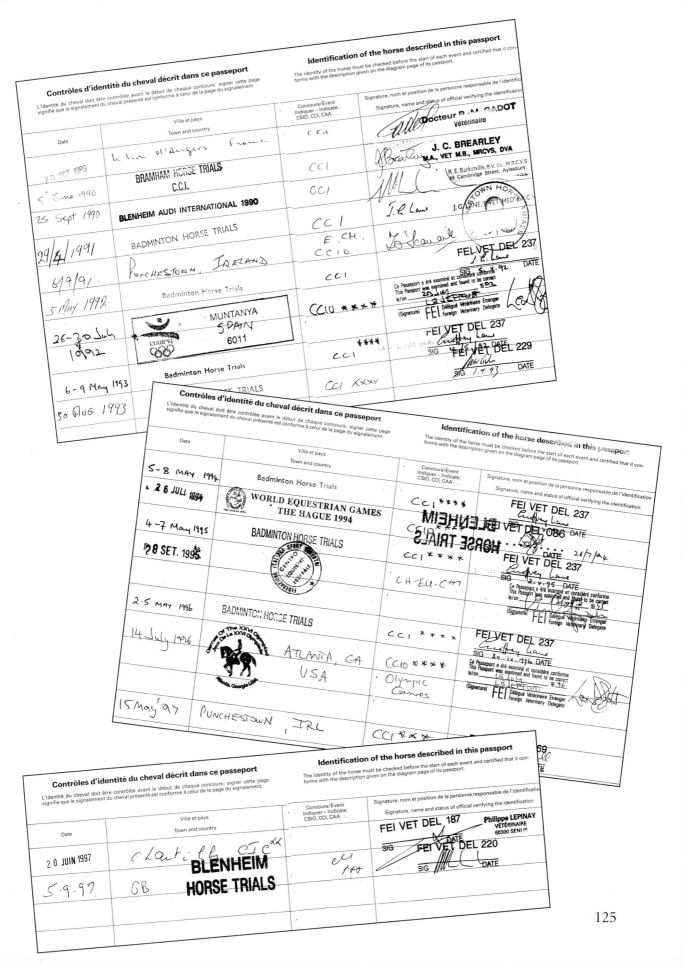

With grateful thanks to everyone who has helped William and me achieve our eventing successes and to Anne Plume for her part in recording William's story.

Specially commissioned photography taken at Salcombe Regis by Kit Houghton

PICTURE ACKNOWLEDGEMENTS

Iain Burns, pp1, 68-9, 78–9, 82 (btm), 86, 87, 88, 90 (btm), 94, 95, 98, 100, 120; Graham Harrison/Clive Richardson Communications Limited, pp2–3; *Bristol Evening Post*, p4; Annie Collings, pp5, 27 (btm), 70 (btm), 72; Russell Cheyne, photograph © Telegraph Group Limited, London, 1993, p6; Kit Houghton, pp7, 9, 14–15, 19, 27 (top), 30–1, 32, 34, 35 (top & btm), 36, 49, 54, 62 (top & btm right), 64, 77, 82 (top), 90 (top), 91, 99 (btm), 102, 103, 106 (top & btm), 107, 110, 111 (top & btm), 113, 114–15, 115 (inset), 117, 118 (top & btm), 119, 122, 123 (top & btm); Clive Boursnell/*Country Life* Picture Library, p10; Hugo M. Czerny, pp11, 43 (top); Stephen Sparkes, pp12–13, 38; unknown source, p22 (top); Equestrian Services Thorney, p22 (btm), 23; Sara Rance, pp26, 42; Srdja Djukanovic, pp39, 46; Nick Morris, pp43 (btm), 75 (top, centre & btm); Trevor Meeks/*Horse & Hound*, pp50, 59, 60, 66 (top); David Miller, p51; Bob Langrish, pp55, 70 (top); Keith Simpson, p60; Shaw-Shot, p61; Richard Mobbs, p62 (btm left); Popperfoto/Reuters, p63; J-B. de Monléon – France, pp67, 71; Trevor Meeks/*Eventing*, p74; Nick Gill, p82 (centre); *Horse & Hound* and *Eventing* front covers, pp96–7; Badminton programme covers reproduced by kind permission of Mitsubishi Motors and the Badminton Horse Trials Committee, pp96–7; *Horse and Pony*, p101; David Davies/Action Plus Photography, pp126–7

Other photographs from the author's collection: pp18, 37 (all), 45, 47, 58, 62 (btm left), 66 (btm left & right), 83, 89, 99 (top, centre left & centre right)

A DAVID & CHARLES BOOK

First published in the UK in 1998

Copyright © David & Charles 1998

Mary King has asserted her right to be identified as author of this work in accordance with the Copyright, Designs and Patents Act, 1988.

A catalogue record for this book is available from the British Library.

ISBN 0 7153 0844 0

Printed in Italy by New Interlitho SpA
for David & Charles
Brunel House   Newton Abbot   Devon